Quarto is the authority on a wide range of topics.

Quarto educates, entertains and enriches the lives of our readers—enthusiasts and lovers of hands-on living. www.quartoknows.com

First published in 2016 by Voyageur Press, an imprint of Quarto Publishing Group USA Inc., 400 First Avenue North, Suite 400, Minneapolis, MN 55401 USA. Telephone: (612) 344-8100
Fax: (612) 344-8692

quartoknows.com
Visit our blogs at quartoknows.com

Voyageur Press titles are also available at discounts in bulk quantity for industrial or sales-promotional use. For details contact the Special Sales Manager at Quarto Publishing Group USA Inc., 400 First Avenue North, Suite 400, Minneapolis, MN 55401 USA.

10 9 8 7 6 5 4 3 2 1

ISBN: 978-0-7603-4970-0

Library of Congress Cataloging-in-Publication Data

Names: Moss, Elliott, 1980- author.
Title: Buxton Hall Barbecue's book of smoke : wood-smoked meat, sides, and more / Elliott Moss.
Description: Minneapolis, MN : Voyageur Press, 2016. | Includes index.
Identifiers: LCCN 2016012188 | ISBN 9780760349700 (hc)
Subjects: LCSH: Barbecuing. | Side dishes (Cooking) | Buxton Hall Barbecue (Asheville, N.C.) | LCGFT: Cookbooks.
Classification: LCC TX840.B3 M677 2016 | DDC 641.7/6--dc23
LC record available at https://lccn.loc.gov/2016012188

Acquiring Editor: Thom O'Hearn
Project Manager: Caitlin Fultz
Art Director and Cover Design: Cindy Samargia Laun
Book Design and Layout: Amy Sly
Photo Stylist: Charlotte L. Autry

Photographs on page 77 and 81 by Elliott Moss

Printed in China

Buxton Hall BBQ

BOOK OF SMOKE

WOOD-SMOKED MEAT, SIDES, AND MORE

ELLIOTT MOSS

VOYAGEUR
PRESS

BUXTON HALL BBQ

BUXTON HALL BBQ

House
slushie
try one, it'll make your day!
PEACH-NEHi,
RASS, TEQUILA

DRAFT BEER

CATAWBA CREAM...	...MT. PORTER
OSKAR BLUES DALE'S P...	...STCROOK RYE PALE
WICKED WEED TYRANNY RED IPA	PISGAH GREYBEARD IPA
GREENMAN ESB	
BOOTUM BROWN ALE	

KEG COCKTAILS

| FAMILY TRADITIONS | COUNTY FAIR |

WELCOME TO BUXTON HALL BARBECUE

In February 2013, I had just been nominated for a James Beard Best Chef Southeast award and I was planning my first restaurant as an owner: Buxton was just getting off the ground when, in a matter of months, everything came crashing down. I parted ways with my business associates and found myself out of a job. I didn't have a kitchen for the first time in years. I wasn't sure what was going to happen or if—never mind when—my break would come. My wife and I considered moving to the desert to escape.

It was frustrating, maybe the most frustrating time in my life. I'd worked hard over the past decade to open and establish two restaurants that weren't mine. First, there was the Whig, a dive bar with an overachieving bar menu in Columbia, South Carolina. When I landed that job, I was just a glorified home cook. I remember having them over to my house and cooking Mexican food late at night, as sort of an audition, and thinking, "Please, give me a chance." The food wasn't supposed to be anything serious. It was extra money for a bar business. But I did get that job and the food grew along with my skills as a chef. We must have been doing something right because the Whig was soon one of the most popular dives in town. It's still popular today.

In 2007, one of the partners from the Whig talked me into moving to Asheville. They were planning to open another bar and restaurant and thought the up-and-coming mountain town was a good fit. I wasn't into the idea at first. Opening a restaurant was the hardest work I'd ever done, and without exaggerating I can say that opening the Whig had been the worst year of my life. And yet, through the mysterious logic of restaurant life, I let them talk me into it. I travelled to Asheville and found that there was a lot to like about life there.

One of the first restaurants I noticed when I moved to Asheville was 12 Bones Smokehouse. They were different from all the barbecue places I grew up with and knew of in South Carolina. They changed their side dishes all the time, which I thought was just brilliant. So many barbecue places treat sides as the same old stuff. Most either turn out mediocre food, never change the sides, or both. But here was 12 Bones with pimento cheese grits, smoked potato salad—really *good* food served on the plate as a side. They had staples, sure, but there were new ideas and new sides all the time. I think that may have been what got me started on thinking about barbecue as a restaurant concept that I could make my own.

We ended up calling the new place the Admiral, and the concept was originally the same as the Whig: a dive bar with "Whatever Elliott wants to do." I remember early on when it was just me in the kitchen and we'd have less than $100 in food sales. Six months later, we were packing the house with $100 tables and people were there for the food. Yet, even while we were figuring out the Admiral—I would say as soon as six months into opening it—I was dreaming of opening my own barbecue restaurant. So when one of the owners approached me about opening another restaurant, I immediately started seeing the run-down white gas station across the street with new eyes: it could be my own barbecue joint.

Then, as quick as if you snapped your fingers, five years went by and the dream was still a

dream. We worked the Admiral into one of the top restaurants in Asheville, a destination. Maybe it was because they were afraid of losing me, but eventually my potential partner decided to open a restaurant with another local chef. I felt like that was when the dream in its original form died.

Another friend and restauranteur didn't want to see my dream die so easily though. Over late nights, we formed the initial plans for a restaurant on Banks Avenue, down the street from where we are now. We researched the plot of land and found that it used to be called Buxton Hill—we thought that was pretty neat and started calling our dream Buxton Hill Barbecue.

You would think that was that, yet we still needed to lock down the location for Buxton and there was so much planning to do. So my partner invited me

ALL IN THE FAMILY

Buxton came about because of my own history with barbecue, which is something deeply ingrained in my family.

Hubert Moore, my mom's dad, actually cooked whole hogs very similar to the way we do it. And boy was he a character: driving around in big, crazy-colored Cadillacs, wearing a seafoam green suit with a Stetson hat, bolo tie, and big diamond rings. Basically, think of J. R. Ewing from the TV show *Dallas* and you can picture his style. He also raised pigs on his own farm, not really as a business but more to feed the family. I don't have much memory of it, but everyone talks about his mom, my great-grandmother, and how good a cook she was. Her hash is legendary. And she's the one who passed down the knowledge of how to use every part of the pig—right up to making head cheese.

Every Saturday he would pick me up in his big Cadillac. We would drive all over back roads together, me and my grandpa. I miss it more and more: those flat expanses of road out there in the backcountry of South Carolina where you just saw corn for miles. We'd go to all sorts of barbecue joints and farms. It was while making rounds with him that I first saw chicken bog (see page 113) being made on a back porch.

My grandfather on my dad's side, R. T. Moss, was not only a good cook; the man knew how to work a fire, for sure. By the time I came around, he was getting on in age, but I heard plenty of stories about folks gathered at his place around a burn barrel and the pit. He would barbecue chickens just about every Friday, and my grandmother would make a big washtub of potato salad. This wasn't just a family affair, either. Back in the day, half the town would stop by for a barbecue plate. The sheriff was there, along with doctors, lawyers, and politicians—everyone would just go hang out, drink some liquor, and eat chicken.

So, as you can see, cooking barbecue and providing a gathering place for the community is definitely something that my dad inherited. He had a welding shop, and he'd use it to create large, custom barbecue grills. He eventually took over the weekly cookout tradition from my grandpa, cooking twenty chickens or more most Fridays. He even had a grand vision of opening a barbecue place. Looking back, I wish he would have done it. He actually got to the point where he thought about doing it on the side, running it out of our house and calling it "Rib-a-Chick" (for ribs and chicken, his specialties). But of course there are health codes and other considerations for actually running any food business, and so eventually he let that dream go.

Even when we weren't cooking barbecue at home, we were often driving and going to barbecue restaurants—whether it was hitting up our favorites or trying to find new spots in the age before the Internet made it so much easier. We went to Brown's and Woody's a lot until they stopped using wood, then we switched to Rodney's. My uncle Danny would get in on it too, bringing us barbecue from farther-away restaurants, like Brown's.

Eventually, our passion for barbecue became less of a pick-up-and-go thing, or a way to a delicious easy dinner, and more of a destination thing. Skeets was one of those places and a huge inspiration to Buxton Hall. It's closed down now due to a feud in the family—that part is not the inspiration—but it was a very cool place. Skeets was located in a very run-down building, maybe half the size of Buxton, with a buffet line that had card tables at the end with plates of banana pudding, red velvet cake, and vanilla cake. What's funny is that the smell of that place is just like Buxton now—the mix of collard vinegar, hush puppies frying, and barbecue. I walk up the stairs and I'm right back at Skeets, surrounded by family.

to take the helm at his other new restaurant for the meantime. Unfortunately, it was a bad fit. What they wanted was again a dive bar with some food on the side while I wanted to aim higher. Our partnership deteriorated to the point where we decided to part ways completely.

It took a leap of faith to walk away from a potentially bad situation, because at the time I had nothing else. I turned to my family for support. I called my dad and told him I needed a grill.

With my new grill, I set up outside a local bar and started to hustle. I'd sell sandwiches late at night. From there, my second family in Asheville started supporting me as well. I was invited by a couple of local artists, Andy Herod and Gabrielle Schafer, to start doing dinners at their house. It turned into a quasi-regular, pop-up type of event. There were eventually tickets and a limit on attendees once word got around.

This, in turn, led to other pop-ups through Asheville's Blind Pig Supper Club and in partnership with other restaurants around town, one of which was MG Road.

This is around the time I met Meherwan Irani, owner of MG Road and eventual partner in Buxton Hall. At the time, I was still feeling pretty burned. I had been promised a lot of things over a number of years and had so much of it fall through. To me, conversations started to seem completely divorced from the reality of what would happen later.

But I was interested in talking with Meherwan. I remember when he opened his first restaurant in Asheville, Chai Pani. I remember eating there and walking away impressed. I also sort of kept running into him. He'd been into the Admiral while I was working there and we crossed paths at Blind Pig events and at a pop-up event in Greenville. At one point, I had hired away one of his cooks.

After everything fell apart for me in 2013, we talked quite a few times and did some events together. I was intrigued when he talked about wanting to open Buxton with me. I was, of course, quite guarded due to my recent history. But his story was very similar to mine. He had very little formal training or background—he just jumped right into a chef's life because he was so passionate about it. For him, it was the food he grew up with in India—the street food that was so nostalgic. For me, it was whole-hog barbecue cooked the way my grandparents used to do it. We both felt strongly about food and tradition, though, and we connected on that level.

So we started planning for Buxton together, just down the street from Buxton Hill in an old skating rink—hence, Buxton Hall. But there were some challenges: rehabbing that old building was going to take time, I was out of a job, and I had also started to recruit cooks who would need work until Buxton opened. Meherwan had an ingenious idea: we'd host pop-up dinners at his bar, MG Road.

Punk Wok came first. It started in December of 2013, and it was the first time I got a chance to work directly with Meherwan. It was also an opportunity for us to both get to know Sarah Cousler, who ended up coming on as sous chef at Buxton (see page 18). Lucky for all of us, Punk Wok was popular from the start. Our first night we sold out of food in three hours, and week after week it was hard to keep up with demand. We eventually had to do it two nights a week instead of one to keep everyone happy!

We kept that going for about a year and then in late 2014 we came up with our next concept, the Thunderbird. This was when we really started gathering our core team for Buxton and began working together on everything from building a menu to executing it. The menu was inspired by the retro country buffets I grew up with in Florence, South Carolina. Some of it was a precursor to what I had in mind for Buxton. In our tiny kitchen, it was a long slog for all of us through that winter. But

it felt like we were all earning our stripes before opening Buxton.

As we neared the opening date for Buxton, we had so many ideas, and I had so many sample menus. I had two spring menus, two summer menus, menus for counter service, menus for table service. Prices were all over the place. Some thoughts were half-formed: "Let's do a big Buxton and a little Buxton sandwich!"

Meherwan helped guide all of this into our opening menu, which was no easy feat. There's no model for what we are at Buxton. We're one part classic barbecue, inspired by the places of my youth, the places that have been there forever. Yet the other part of Buxton is the ambitious food beyond the hogs. We have a group of very talented chefs who came out swinging. So we're driven by the craft of barbecue—being really good, being a pitmaster—it is a craft. But the rest of the menu from the beginning wasn't so simple.

We still operate in a gray area and we're always evolving. What you see in this book and what you'll find on our menu when you come in may not match exactly, because we always try to draw on what's in season and what's exciting to us. You may find some of the sides or some of the desserts strange, a cross between Southern heritage and modern cooking. But our hope is that you'll find new ideas and walk away inspired both by tradition and by some of the new techniques and variations we're putting on the classics.

In short, we hope you enjoy the food you'll find in this book and in our restaurant with an open mind. Barbecue is beautiful, and you should respect it. But just like any craft, or any art, as a creator you have to not be afraid to step off the beaten path. Make your own food and make your own traditions.

Welcome to Buxton Hall Barbecue.

—Elliott Moss

Farm Lun...

from Merietta Buckley
- Florence bakery -

Chicken Bog - Peas + hot sauce
- Pee ... to the low country
es perlo -
... recipe -

Catfish stew - toma... bacon, miripox, spicy

- Cat fish ponds in the
Pee Dee - family Recipe -

chow chow - ten mile farms
vegetables fermented 6 months -
- Just down the road -

spinning chicken (also known as dancing chic...
- Bar-b-cue mop -

Brian Canipeli + I - idea / party

THE CHEFS AND THE FOOD

The team we've put together at Buxton is a big part of our success so far. We all spent months getting on the same page, many of us working together since long before we opened the doors. Then we all went through the trial by fire that is opening a new restaurant, adapting and dialing in until everything was the way we wanted it. And of course, we continue to evolve. There are three chefs in particular who are a big part of the restaurant, and this book, behind the scenes.

SARAH COUSLER: Sarah's mom is from the Philippines and her dad is from the eastern part of North Carolina, so she has a very interesting combination of culinary backgrounds. She has so much history to pull from on both sides, and like me she loves drawing inspiration from her family and her roots. It's funny because even though Sarah is now one of our city's most talented chefs, her mom still barely lets her cook when she goes home! Sarah has further developed the Asian side of her culinary skills with trips to countries like Japan. She's going to be a big part of our future and I'm so excited to see what dishes she comes up with next.

DAN SILO: Dan is from upstate New York. He fell in love with Asheville and packed his knives. In a small-world moment, Dan actually came in to train at the Admiral on my last day there. I was so checked out at that point that I refused to train him! But we ended up getting to know each other socially and he eventually started working with us at the Punk Wok and Thunderbird pop-ups. Dan was a huge part of opening Buxton, and not just the menu. He literally was there doing physical labor, rehabbing the building. He and I also spent long nights cooking hogs, smoking all night and working all day. I think that's a real bonding experience, going through a crazy twenty-four hours like that.

ASHLEY CAPPS: Ashley and I go way back. I'd guess we met sometime in 2008. She had spent time in New York and worked at very highly regarded restaurants, but I was more impressed by what she created. She has a way with desserts—there's no other way to put it—and I desperately wanted to bring her on to run the dessert program at the Admiral. We couldn't afford it, but I always kept Ashley in the back of my mind as I thought about opening my own restaurant. Once I finally got the project back on track, there was nobody else. Her own career had taken her to multiple restaurants in the meantime, including John Fleer's Rhubarb, but the timing worked in our favor. She was ready for a new challenge and she brainstormed and produced Buxton's desserts from the opening menu on.

Then there's me, **ELLIOTT**. As head chef, what's most important to me is honoring the South Carolina barbecue traditions I grew up with. (Yes, I understand that might sound a little weird coming from a North Carolina restaurant.) What I mean by this is that we always take time to do things the right way. Buxton is a whole-hog barbecue restaurant first and foremost, and that means it has an educational component almost every day. We often get questions like "Why can't I order ribs today?" or "Why don't you have brisket?" Well, it's just not the type of barbecue we do.

THE BARBECUE ROAD TRIP

Our inspiration at Buxton, especially for the meat and for the hogs, is to smoke it the original way it was smoked in the Carolinas—meaning cooking whole hogs (no Boston butts!), pit-smoked with wood only. We never use gas. It's really the whole reason I wanted to open Buxton in the first place: to bring all-wood, whole-hog barbecue to Asheville. Before opening Buxton, Meherwan and I took the cooks on a couple of road trips down to Florence and other spots in South Carolina that were important to my barbecue upbringing to show them the roots of this style of barbecue.

Our first stop was True BBQ in Columbia, South Carolina. For much of the team, that was their first taste of South Carolina hash, and it was a great introduction because True's hash is good! This was one of the only stops we made to a newish restaurant, but it was worth it. True also makes very good wood-smoked pork and ribs. We followed that up with Little Pigs BBQ Buffet, a true step back in time to the barbecue buffets of old of my childhood. I just love the setup of these places. They have a huge spread on a table with sauces for the mustard aficionados as well as folks who are vinegar barbecue lovers. And at the end of the line is a table just packed with pies and cakes.

We made a quick pit stop at Maurice's Piggie Park BBQ (see page 29 for more on their famous mustard sauce) and made our way to Florence, where I grew up. This is where we visited the places I remember most from my childhood, such as Woodstone BBQ, Cain's, and Brown's. They are all buffet style, and they all lean toward the vinegar- and pepper-based sauce like the one we use at Buxton. Many also serve regional favorites that I brought to our menu, notably the catfish stew and chicken bog. We also visited the Thunderbird, a country buffet with a weird bar and a huge neon sign. It's the place that served as the inspiration for one of our running pop-ups at MG Road.

While it was important to me to stop at places where I had history, it was bittersweet. So many of these classic barbecue joints have switched from all-wood, whole-hog style barbecues to gas-fired machines. Still, at least I was able to share my memories with the crew, and we could still find those totally unique regional dishes that hold so much nostalgia for me. They are such a big part of what I want to share at Buxton Hall.

Our next stop was in a little town called Hemingway, South Carolina. It's a town that you might not have heard of, but it's huge in the world of whole-hog barbecue. We visited with Rodney Scott and ate at his place, Scott's Bar-B-Que. This stop was night and day with the places that have turned away from wood. Rodney is a living legend who not only cooks whole hog, but also chops his own wood. People drive from all over the Southeast—and even further than that—to visit Rodney's. We also hit up Cooper's Country Store, a legendary place for country ham and hash and a true general store. They're selling everything from guns to plumbing parts!

The trip ended on a high note for sure, as we followed Rodney's with a visit to Skylight Inn BBQ in Ayden, North Carolina. Sam Jones is the man behind Skylight, and he's been doing whole-hog, all-wood-fired barbecue for something like fifty years, keeping it going from his grandfather who ran it before him. The business is still all in his family, and it's really the cornerstone of that community. To me, Sam and Rodney really personify the best of the brotherhood of whole-hog, all-wood barbecue families that are keeping the tradition alive across the Carolinas. Ayden and Hemingway aren't that close, but these guys tease each other like they are next-door neighbors. North Carolina barbecue scholars (I swear that's a real thing) will tell you that if you go back far enough, all Carolina barbecue was made the same way, with whole hogs, cooked on all wood, and dressed with a vinegar sauce. At Buxton, my hope is to be worthy of that brotherhood, keep the whole-hog tradition alive, and maybe extend the next person's road trip just a little farther west.

BACK TO BUXTON

I trust that gives you a sense of the long tradition we're proud to be a part of. To honor that tradition, we use only hardwoods and barbecue pits to smoke our meat and the bulk of our meat is whole-hog barbecue. We get our hogs from Larry Crocher at Vandele Farms. In short: Larry is the man. He raises pastured pigs and they're a big part of our story. Even here, in a city that's very concerned about the food system, it is hard to find pigs raised the right way. Our other meats come from a variety of local suppliers but all of them are places where we know the owners and we've seen how the animals are raised. We usually get our beef from Hickory Nut Gap, for example, a well-known area farm that treats its animals right.

Our wood is also important to mention. Derek Watson supplies our wood and I've been working with him for years. In a way, it's like we're in this business together as the more business Buxton has the more wood we need from Derek. He knows the area very well and he knows just how to process the wood for us. If you have a local barbecue restaurant that runs on wood, chances are it has a similar relationship with someone in your town.

Our sides and our desserts also take inspiration from barbecue traditions, though we do take more of a creative approach with them than with the meat. One of the reasons behind this is that many great barbecue places focus on the meat to the detriment of the sides and desserts. And it works just fine for them: in many places, it *is* all about the pork. The potato salad is rightly an afterthought. However, it fits both Asheville and the personality of our chefs better to create an entire menu that pushes barbecue forward.

We want to take full advantage of our pits and our hogs. We're fortunate to have three pits at the heart of our kitchen, so it's an ongoing experiment in some ways to see how we can make the most of them. Our brussels sprouts, for example, were a natural fit. Why wouldn't you want to place them right beneath the hog, soaking up all that smoke and getting basted with the tasty fat? Another example is our Grits and Gravy (see page 114), where we often smoke the grits and then use the hog bones to make the gravy.

The same thought and consideration that goes into our sides also goes into our desserts—maybe even more so thanks to the nonstop mind of Ashley (see page 19). Never content to do something the easy way, Ashley makes everything possible from scratch and turns old ideas into new desserts. Take the Banana Pudding Pie: I told Ashley in no uncertain terms that we needed banana pudding on the menu, somehow, some way. I figured she'd turn out an amazing banana pudding, but she took it even further. She transformed that iconic dessert into a pie that was immediately a huge hit with our customers. From top to bottom, from the house-made vanilla wafer crust to the brown sugar meringue, you can see Ashley's genius at work.

So that's who we are and this is where we're coming from. In the chapters that follow, you'll find recipes that all come from this viewpoint, rooted in tradition but often made new in our own way.

RUBS AND SAUCES

I've already talked a bit about the importance of sourcing good-quality meat, but the other ingredients you use are equally important for different reasons. Hot sauces are a good example. I grew up on Texas Pete, so we use that in just about every recipe that calls for hot sauce. If you switch to Tabasco or Cholula, you're going to get a different result. Same goes for something as subtle as mayonnaise (we recommend Duke's).

With that in mind, the next few pages will walk you through our own house sauces and rubs. These sauces go with almost all of the meats in this book, and the Hog Sauce is key to the whole hog in particular. But as with any cookbook, try these recipes and then, if you like, use them as a starting point to create your own flavors.

HOG SAUCE (VINEGAR/PEPPER SAUCE)

YIELD: About 1 gallon

- ½ gallon cider vinegar
- ½ gallon white distilled vinegar
- ½ cup finely ground red pepper
- 2 tablespoons crushed red pepper
- ¼ cup finely ground black pepper
- ½ cup sugar
- 2 lemons, halved, wrapped in cheesecloth

NOTE: Yield is large enough for a whole hog. Typically, you'll season the hog with about ½ gallon when you pull it and add additional sauce to taste or as needed when serving and eating the pulled pork.

If I could have it my way, I would be a barbecue dictator: people would only be able to eat barbecued pork with this sauce. At the very least, when people come to Buxton, I want them to try it before they try any other sauce—especially red sauce! Now, I know that we don't have the deep-rooted community of folks who grew up eating vinegar-based barbecue in western Carolina, but my hope is that we stake some ground here and in twenty years everyone will be eating it.

The recipe that follows isn't quite as spicy as I personally like my sauce; however, it is the level of spice that we found works best for most people. If you like spicier barbecue, by all means ramp up the peppers in the sauce. One other note: most East Carolina vinegar sauces don't use sugar, but I really like it in this sauce. Hey, I'm not claiming to be an East Carolina barbecue restaurant either! This is Buxton's sauce, and it just happens to be a vinegar-based one.

PREPARATION
Combine all ingredients in a large pot. Bring to a low simmer and cook for 20 minutes. Turn off the heat. Remove the lemons and let the mixture cool.

This sauce can be packaged back inside the vinegar jugs or any containers with tight-fitting lids. In the fridge, it will keep for close to a year.

RED BARBECUE SAUCE

YIELD: About 3 cups

- 1¼ cups ketchup
- 2 tablespoons prepared yellow mustard
- ½ cup Hog Sauce (page 24)
- ½ cup Hog Stock (page 32), or another stock or water
- ¾ teaspoon onion powder
- ¾ teaspoon garlic powder
- ¾ teaspoon ground black pepper
- 1 tablespoon sugar
- ¼ teaspoon hickory smoke powder (optional)
- 2 tablespoons honey
- 2 tablespoons light brown sugar
- 2 tablespoons molasses
- 2 tablespoons Texas Pete hot sauce
- 1½ teaspoons Worcestershire sauce
- 1½ teaspoons soy sauce

The red sauce we make at Buxton came from my family recipes. I must have pored through ten or more variations on chicken and rib sauces and experimented to come up with our final recipe. The trickiest part is that many called for Coleman's hot sauce as an ingredient. It was always in my fridge while growing up, but it's still a regional sauce and one I couldn't source in Asheville. I had to retool recipes to work around that. The final version is what you see here, and it's about as close as I could get to the flavor of my family's homemade sauce.

Whatever you do, please don't fill a sauce bottle with this and squeeze it cold onto your meat. This sauce is meant to be served warm and at a thinner consistency than most red sauces. If your sauce gets thick during the warming process, or if you accidentally warm it too long, you can water it down a bit without compromising the flavor. Or you can add Hog Sauce (page 24), which will thin it down and change the flavor in a way that I personally like even better.

PREPARATION

Combine all ingredients in a medium sauce pot. Simmer for 20 minutes and then remove from the heat. This sauce will keep in the fridge for 1 week, but you should serve it warm.

WHITE BARBECUE SAUCE

YIELD: About 1½ cups

DRY INGREDIENTS

- ½ teaspoon garlic powder
- ½ teaspoon onion powder
- ½ teaspoon hickory smoke powder (available from Terra Spice or a specialty spice store)
- ½ teaspoon kosher salt
- ½ teaspoon ground black pepper
- 4 teaspoons sugar

WET INGREDIENTS

- 1 teaspoon Worcestershire sauce
- 1 teaspoon fresh lemon juice
- 1 teaspoon Texas Pete hot sauce
- 2 teaspoons cider vinegar
- 2 teaspoons water
- 1 cup mayonnaise (preferably Duke's)

I didn't grow up with white sauce, but ever since I discovered it, I have loved it. If you like mayonnaise, what's not to love? When I was opening Buxton, I knew I needed a white sauce—not for the pork, but for chicken and for anything fried. (I've noticed some people do enjoy it with the pork, but I just can't recommend using it that way.) This sauce is great with many of the other smoked meats in the book, though—definitely try it with the turkey and the chicken. Keep some on hand for next time you make french fries too!

PREPARATION

Place all the dry ingredients in a large mixing bowl and stir to combine.

Combine all the wet ingredients except for the mayonnaise in another bowl. Add the wet ingredient mixture to the dry ingredients while whisking to incorporate. (Whisking will help keep the dry ingredients from clumping.) Add the mayonnaise and whisk until it's incorporated.

Store in a jar with tight-fitting lid and refrigerate. It will keep for up to 2 weeks.

MUSTARD SAUCE

YIELD: About 3 cups

DRY INGREDIENTS

- 1½ teaspoons onion powder
- 1½ teaspoons garlic powder
- ¼ teaspoon smoke powder
- 1½ teaspoons finely ground black pepper
- 2 tablespoons sugar

WET INGREDIENTS

- 2 tablespoons lemon juice
- 2 tablespoons Louisiana-style hot sauce (like Texas Pete)
- 2 tablespoons Worcestershire sauce
- 2 cups prepared yellow mustard (preferably French's)
- 1 tablespoon tomato paste
- 2 tablespoons honey

The mustard sauce I remember from South Carolina was made famous by Maurice Bessinger, who owned a barbecue joint called Piggie Park. Eventually he built up a huge barbecue empire and his sauce was available at grocery stores all over the state. But Maurice was also a contentious personality and he lost some of those important relationships before he died. These days, his children carry on his restaurant. His siblings opened their own barbecue place called Bessinger's, with a very similar sauce.

Many of the barbecue joints known for their mustard sauces became famous by using honey in the sauce—only to switch to a cheaper sweetener once they could afford to coast on their name. I am a big believer in using real honey in this type of sauce, though, as it produces a more complex flavor and a silkier texture.

PREPARATION

Combine the dry ingredients in a large mixing bowl. Add the lemon juice, hot sauce, and Worcestershire sauce, then whisk to combine. Make sure to whisk well enough so that the mixture doesn't have clumps. Whisk in the mustard, tomato paste, and honey.

Store in a jar with a tight-fitting lid and refrigerate. It will keep for up to 1 month.

RIB RUB

YIELD: 7 cups

- 4 cups packed light brown sugar
- 1½ cups kosher salt
- ½ cup ground red pepper
- ¼ cup ground cumin
- ¼ cup ground black pepper
- 2 tablespoons garlic powder
- 2 tablespoons onion powder
- 1 tablespoon herbes de Provence
- 1 tablespoon crushed red pepper
- 1 tablespoon dry mustard
- 1 tablespoon ground fennel
- 1 teaspoon ground cinnamon

I'm the first to admit that compared to other pitmasters, I am a whole-hog guy before I'm a rib guy. In fact, I didn't eat ribs much growing up, which might be why my take on them is a little different. For example, many people don't put sugar in their rib rubs, but I like it. This rub also works well on pork butt or even chicken as an alternative to the chicken rub that follows.

PREPARATION

Place all the ingredients in a medium-size mixing bowl and stir until incorporated. You can also put all the ingredients in a food processor and pulse until incorporated.

Store the mixture in a resealable plastic bag or an airtight container for up to 1 month.

CHICKEN RUB

YIELD: About 5 cups

- 2 cups packed light brown sugar
- 1 cup granulated sugar
- 1 cup salt
- ½ cup ground white pepper
- ¼ cup garlic powder
- ¼ cup onion powder
- ¼ cup ground red pepper
- ¼ cup dried oregano
- 3 tablespoons ground cumin
- 2 teaspoons rubbed sage
- 2 teaspoons ground coriander

This is similar to the rib rub, but of course, for my palate, the spices are more suitable for poultry. This is my go-to rub for barbecue chicken and you'll find that it's great on other poultry and light meats as well.

PREPARATION

Place all the ingredients in a medium-size mixing bowl and stir until incorporated. You can also put all the ingredients in a food processor and pulse until incorporated.

Store the mixture in a resealable plastic bag or an airtight container for up to 1 month.

HOG STOCK

YIELD: 5 gallons

- Bones, cartilage, and fatty bits from one barbecued hog
- About 5 pounds of vegetable scraps, or 5 unpeeled onions, halved; 5 unpeeled carrots, halved; and 2 heads of celery, roughly chopped
- 2 bunches fresh parsley
- 2 bunches fresh thyme
- 2 heads garlic, split apart
- 10 bay leaves
- 3 tablespoons whole peppercorns
- 2 tablespoons kosher salt
- Cold water

When you cook whole hogs, you end up with a lot of hog bones at the end of the day. Like many restaurants, we are left with a lot of veggie peels and onion skins as well. Our Hog Stock has been with us from the start as a way to get the most from those bones and scraps. It's a great base flavor to add to many of our sides and sauces. I'm not going to lie: I've tried substituting Hog Stock in place of water in just about every recipe I could think of except for our desserts!

At home, you will need to borrow a large pot (try a friend who homebrews or fries turkeys) to make such a large batch of stock. Of course, you can scale this recipe down. The idea is that you'll be working with a whole hog's worth of bones, but you may very well have just a half hog or even less. As for the vegetables, follow the recipe or start saving veggie scraps a few weeks ahead of when you plan to make the stock by saving them in a plastic bag stored in the freezer. There's no need to use fresh, whole vegetables.

PREPARATION

In a very large stock pot, add bones and bits and vegetables along with herbs and spices. Cover with cold water. Bring to a boil and reduce to a simmer. Continue to simmer for up to 8 hours. Skim the fat during cooking. Remove as many solids from the pot as possible. This will help with straining. Let cool to room temperature. In batches, strain through a fine mesh strainer. Use immediately or freeze.

This stock is a great base for soups, gravies, and dishes like collards. It's also delicious sipped straight as bone broth.

QUICK SMOKING

A QUICK NOTE ON QUICK SMOKING

Now that I co-own a restaurant with multiple built-in pits, I have no need for workarounds that add smoke flavor. If something needs a hit of smoke, it goes next to the hog or on the hog, or it's hung above the smoker for more of a cold-smoked character.

Yet I realize that not everyone has the ability, time, or energy to take on building a pit (which we'll cover in the next chapter). For years, I also used the quick-smoking information in this chapter to create dishes in the restaurant kitchens where I worked. While you can't beat true pit flavor, you'd be surprised how effective a quick smoking can be. And it takes such a minimal investment of time and money that there's really no reason not to give yourself the smoked pork you crave or impress your friends with a batch of smoked wings.

The main project in the pages that follows is a hotel pan smoker setup. It's not only inexpensive to put together, but it's large enough to handle decent-size cuts of meat as well. Sure, you won't be doing a whole hog, but that's not the point! You can quickly add the smoke flavor you want to pork butt or ribs. And by using a combination of a smoker and the oven, you turn what's normally a full-day or even full-weekend project into something that resembles preparing a normal meal. It's also a great way to start learning about different wood characteristics and how different-size cuts of meat absorb smoke flavor at different rates. When you're smoking for minutes instead of hours, the time investment makes experimentation much easier and less risky. Once you dial in and get comfortable, you can always give the pit a try—you'll be that much the wiser for having quick-smoked meat first.

The hotel pan smoker will do you right in just about any kitchen, but it's not truly portable. To that end, I'm also including a hack for a Girl Scout mess kit. With just a drill, you can turn one of these classic mess kits—easy to find online—into the perfect campfire smoker. While you can't fit a lot inside, there's no denying that smoked foods and the great outdoors just go together. Now you can smoke just about anywhere—but remember to put out your fire.

THE TABLETOP SMOKER

YOU WILL NEED

- Wood chips, 2 handfuls (I like a mix of hickory and apple—see page 42)
- Water, cider vinegar, or beer
- 6-inch-deep, full-size aluminum hotel pan (see Note)
- 2½-inch-deep, full-size aluminum perforated hotel pan (see Note)
- Heavy-duty aluminum foil
- Gas burner (like a turkey fryer burner or a side burner on a gas grill)
- Oven, range, or gas grill along with a resting rack or wire rack and cookie sheet to finish cooking (depending on what you're smoking)

NOTE: You can buy hotel pans online through www.amazon.com or www.webstaurantstore.com for around $35 plus shipping. If you have a local restaurant supply store, it will carry them, but they will probably cost a little more.

A tabletop smoker is an inexpensive and easy-to-build tool you can use to smoke great Boston butt, chicken, fish, vegetables, or really anything that will fit inside. Tabletop smoking is a pretty forgiving process as well, as you will actually be applying smoke only for a short period of time and finishing the cooking with an easy-to-manage heat source like an oven.

While it's called a tabletop smoker, you'll still want to set it up on a table that's outdoors unless you're in a commercial kitchen or have a gas stove and a very, very powerful hood. Just be warned: it will produce a lot of smoke! Once you get the idea of how the tabletop smoking method works, feel free to play around and experiment with different foods. It's a lot of fun.

GETTING STARTED

Soak your wood chips for 20 minutes. Water will work just fine, but you can also use cider vinegar or your favorite beer—the wood chips will produce some steam early on and a flavored liquid will add some additional essence to your meat or vegetables.

After the chips are soaked, drain the excess liquid and place the chips in a small pile inside the 6-inch hotel pan. Then place the perforated hotel pan inside the 6-inch pan.

Place your seasoned meat or vegetables on top of the perforated pan—the food can just rest on the pan and does not need to fit inside it. Make sure that you leave plenty of the holes uncovered by the food. The smoke will come through the holes to surround the food, so if you're smoking a lot of something that would nest inside the pan, say chicken wings, you'll want to do them in batches in order to keep enough of the holes clear.

After the meat or vegetables have gone in, wrap the top and sides of the pan tightly with heavy-duty foil. You don't want any spaces uncovered where smoke can come out the side. (This might take 2 or 3 large sheets of foil.) Once the pan is covered up, cut a quarter-size hole in the top. This will be the vent for the smoke.

Place the pan on a gas burner, doing your best to line up the burner to where the wood chips are inside the pan. Turn the burner to high. Once you see smoke—it won't take very long—turn the burner to low. You want to see a light stream of smoke coming out of the vent. If it seems to be smoking too much, turn off the gas, wait a few minutes, and then return the gas to low heat. This is where you can play around and experiment. It might be that a little higher level of heat and a bit more intense smoke is what works for you . . . like I said before, this is a pretty forgiving method of smoking.

If the smoke turns a yellowish color, the chips are spent. This smoke produces an acrid, bitter taste, so it's best to avoid smoking with spent chips. If you see yellow smoke, remove the foil and perforated pan with a grill glove or dry towel (the pans will be very hot). Remove the old wood chips and add fresh ones. Place the perforated pan back inside, wrap with foil, and continue the smoking.

As for how long you smoke the food, see the guide on page 42 or the recipes in this chapter for recommended quick-smoking and oven-finishing times.

QUICK GUIDE FOR MEATS AND VEGETABLES

BOSTON BUTT 30 minutes of smoke, then 5 hours in oven (covered in foil) at 220°F followed by 5 hours in oven (uncovered) at 220°F

SPARERIBS 20 minutes of smoke, then 5 hours in the oven (covered in foil) at 220°F followed by 90 minutes in the oven (uncovered) at 220°F

BABY BACK RIBS 20 minutes of smoke, then 4 hours in the oven (covered in foil) at 220°F followed by 90 minutes in the oven (uncovered) at 220°F

CHICKEN OR TURKEY WINGS OR DRUMSTICKS 10 minutes of smoke, then deep-fry for 5 to 10 minutes

MUSHROOMS 5 minutes of smoke, season, then sauté or grill to your liking

VEGETABLES 5 minutes of smoke, season, then sauté or grill to your liking

Browse through this chapter for some of my favorite recipes featuring the tabletop smoker. I'd recommend trying one of those recipes first because they contain complete instructions. After that, maybe you will want to go off the beaten path. If that's the case, use the guide to cook times at left as a ballpark.

Typically, for Boston butts and larger cuts like brisket, you will want to smoke for around 30 minutes. Smaller cuts of meat, like ribs and whole chickens, can pick up substantial smoke flavor in about 15 minutes. Even smaller foods or foods with delicate flavors, such as fish, chicken wings, and vegetables, can smoke for around 5 to 10 minutes. And remember, whatever you smoke will have to be finished either in the oven (low and slow), on the grill, or on the stovetop in a pan.

WOOD CHOICES

Hickory wood chips are easy to find and a great choice for tabletop smoking. Apple wood is a bit harder to source, but it also works really well. As I'm in Carolina and not Texas, I've rarely used mesquite, but if you know you like that flavor, go ahead and give it a try. Another recommendation is to talk to the people in your area who cut wood for a living. They often have access to tons of wood chips looking for a home. Do some research on the fruit or nut trees in your area. Many are suitable for smoking.

THE GIRL SCOUT MESS KIT SMOKER

YOU WILL NEED

- Drill with ¼-inch drill bit
- 1 Girl Scout mess kit
- Wood chips, 1 handful (see page 42)
- Water, cider vinegar, or beer
- Campfire or gas burner (like a turkey fryer burner or a side burner on a gas grill)

While the tabletop smoker is my go-to tool for most quick-smoking tasks, there's something to be said for a truly portable smoker. Maybe you love to fish and want to smoke that fresh-caught trout right at camp. Or maybe you're more of a forager and you just gathered some delicious mushrooms. Either way, by packing a slightly modified version of the classic Girl Scout mess kit, you can both smoke and fry your foods while adding very little weight to your pack.

Girl Scout mess kits such as the one shown here pop up all the time at thrift stores, but you can also find them online at sites like eBay. They're usually about ten dollars.

BUILD THE SMOKER

Using your drill and a steady work surface, drill one hole in the center of the mess kit frying pan's bottom. Drill two additional holes below and two above.

Working around the circle, continue to drill two holes between the center hole and the edge of the pan. You want about fifteen to twenty evenly spaced holes when you're finished.

Next, drill three holes in the center of the frying pan's lid.

USING THE SMOKER

Using the mess kit smoker is just like using a small version of the tabletop smoker. Start by soaking your wood chips for 20 minutes using water, cider vinegar, or beer.

After the chips are soaked, drain the excess liquid and place the chips in a small pile inside of the sauce pot part of the kit. Then place the perforated frying pan on top of the pot.

Now you're ready to place your food inside the smoker. When doing so, make sure not to completely cover all the holes. The smoke will come through the holes to surround the food. Once the food is inside, place the lid on the frying pan.

Carefully place the entire setup over your fire or burner until the chips start smoking. Once you see smoke—it won't take very long—turn the burner to low or raise the pan up so it's receiving less heat from the fire. You want to see a light stream of smoke coming out of the vent. If it seems to be smoking too much, remove the pan from the heat, wait a few minutes, and then place it back over the fire.

You probably won't smoke anything in this smoker so long that you see the smoke turn a yellowish color. However, if this happens, the chips are spent and will add an acrid flavor to your food. Switch out your chips before smoking any further.

Once you've finished smoking, you can clean out the saucepan that the chips were in and use it to cook your food.

BOSTON BUTT (PULLED PORK)

YIELD: 6 to 8 servings (about 5 pounds)

SMOKE TIME: 30 minutes

COOK TIME: 10 hours

- Fresh Boston butt (preferably bone-in as it adds more flavor), about 5 pounds
- 2 cups Rib Rub (page 30)

NOTE: I like using the Rib Rub, as the brown sugar adds a nice bark. However, other rubs can work well. Play around!

- 1 cup Hog Sauce (page 24), for finishing

EQUIPMENT

- Large bowl
- Tabletop smoker
- Heavy-duty foil
- Wire resting rack
- Sheet pan
- Rubber gloves

Most of the pulled pork you find in barbecue joints comes from the cut called Boston butt. However, there's a wide variety of preparation techniques. I find using a brown sugar–based rub during the smoking and cooking creates a nice bark on the surface that acts as a flavorful, protective exterior and locks in the juices—which keeps the pork from drying out. You can sauce up the finished pork however you'd like, but I recommend using the Hog Sauce (page 24). The vinegar in the sauce mixes with the fatty drippings and emulsifies, creating a sort of meat-based vinaigrette. For one butt, about a cup of Hog Sauce should do it.

PREPARATION

Rinse and towel dry the Boston butt. Place it in a large bowl and generously apply the Rib Rub. Place the bowl in the refrigerator, uncovered, for about 8 hours or overnight. As it sits, the rub almost acts like a cure and will produce a deeper, richer flavor. The salt in the rub will draw out moisture from the butt as well.

Once you're ready to smoke, preheat your oven to 220°F and get your tabletop smoker going. (Follow the Getting Started section of the tabletop smoking method on page 40) Remove the butt from the fridge and place it in the smoker. Smoke the butt for 30 minutes. Remove the butt from the smoker and wrap it in heavy-duty foil. Place the butt on a wire rack set inside a sheet pan. Put the butt in the oven and cook for 5 hours. Remove the butt from the oven and take away the foil. Place the butt back on the baking rack. Continue to cook for about 5 more hours or until the internal temperature is between 180°F and 205°F and the outside has a nice bark.

recipe continues

FINISHING AND SERVING

Remove the butt from the oven. Carefully pour off any juice and fat from the sheet pan into a large bowl. Place both the bowl and the butt, still on the sheet pan, in the refrigerator to cool. Rest the butt in the fridge for 30 minutes. This will let the meat cool down enough to handle and it will also let the natural juices settle into the meat.

After 30 minutes, remove the juice and fat from refrigerator, skim the fat, and pour the juices into a large bowl. Now remove the butt. Work within a pan that will catch the juices, or use a cutting board designed to catch excess drippings. With rubber gloves, remove the bone from the butt—it should pull right out.

Now pull apart the meat with your hands. It should be pretty easy. This is where your personal preference comes in: you can leave the pork in big chunks, continue to hand shred, or use a cleaver to chop up the pork. No matter how you pull or chop, place the processed meat in the large bowl of drippings and lightly salt to taste.

Add the Hog Sauce and mix with your hands to incorporate.

At this point, the world is your oyster, but here's what I recommend: layer the pork on a nice soft bun or two slices or white bread, adding extra Hog Sauce and some sweet coleslaw.

The rest of the meat will keep for about 5 days in the refrigerator. To serve, heat on the stove over medium heat, moistening with additional Hog Sauce or water as needed.

CURED, SMOKED BACON

![spatula icon] **YIELD:** 4½ pounds of bacon

![flame icon] **SMOKE TIME:** 20 to 30 minutes

![timer icon] **COOK TIME:** 2 hours

FOR THE CURE

- 1 cup salt
- ⅓ cup granulated sugar
- ⅓ cup brown sugar
- 12 dried bay leaves, crushed
- 1 tablespoon whole white peppercorn, crushed
- 1 small bunch fresh thyme

FOR THE BACON

- 5 pounds fresh pork belly, skinned

EQUIPMENT

- Bowl
- Large nonreactive container, such as a plastic food storage container
- Tabletop smoker
- Wire resting rack
- Sheet pan or cookie sheet

Making your own bacon is surprisingly easy, and the results are so much better than what you find at the grocery store. The hardest part may actually be finding the pork belly you need to make it! But call around town and visit your local butcher. Be sure to request it with the skin off and let them know you want fresh pork belly for bacon.

This hot-smoked recipe is designed to fully cook the bacon, so it will actually be safe to eat as soon as you're done baking—though bacon is best fried! (This is in contrast to cold-smoked bacon.) And while this recipe was written for the tabletop smoker, you can make bacon on the pit as well. Just make sure to smoke it until the internal temperature is 145°F.

PREPARATION

Combine all the cure ingredients except for the thyme in a bowl. Dredge the pork belly in the cure liberally, turning and rubbing to ensure it's evenly coated. Line the bottom of a nonreactive container with a dusting of the remaining cure and the thyme sprigs.

Place the pork belly in the container, cover, and refrigerate for 3 days. During this time, flip the belly over about once per day to ensure the wet brine that has formed in the container is evenly distributed.

Continue to let the belly cure in the fridge, turning one time per day, for another 3 to 4 days. Check for firmness: fully cured pork belly will be firm to the touch at its thickest point—it should feel similar to a cooked pork chop. Once the belly feels firm to the touch, remove from the cure and thoroughly rinse. Allow to dry, uncovered, overnight in the refrigerator.

When you're ready to smoke and cook the bacon, preheat your oven to 200°F. Follow the Getting Started section of the tabletop smoking method (page 40). Remove the cured pork belly from the fridge and smoke for 20 minutes. If you like really smoky bacon, smoke for a full 30 minutes.

Place the belly on the wire resting rack nested on top of the sheet pan. Cook the belly at 200°F for 2 to 3 hours, or until the internal temperature at its thickest point reaches 145°F.

Cool the bacon in the refrigerator for 2 to 3 hours or until completely cooled. The bacon is ready to slice and fry to your liking. Use within 1 week or slice and freeze the remaining portions.

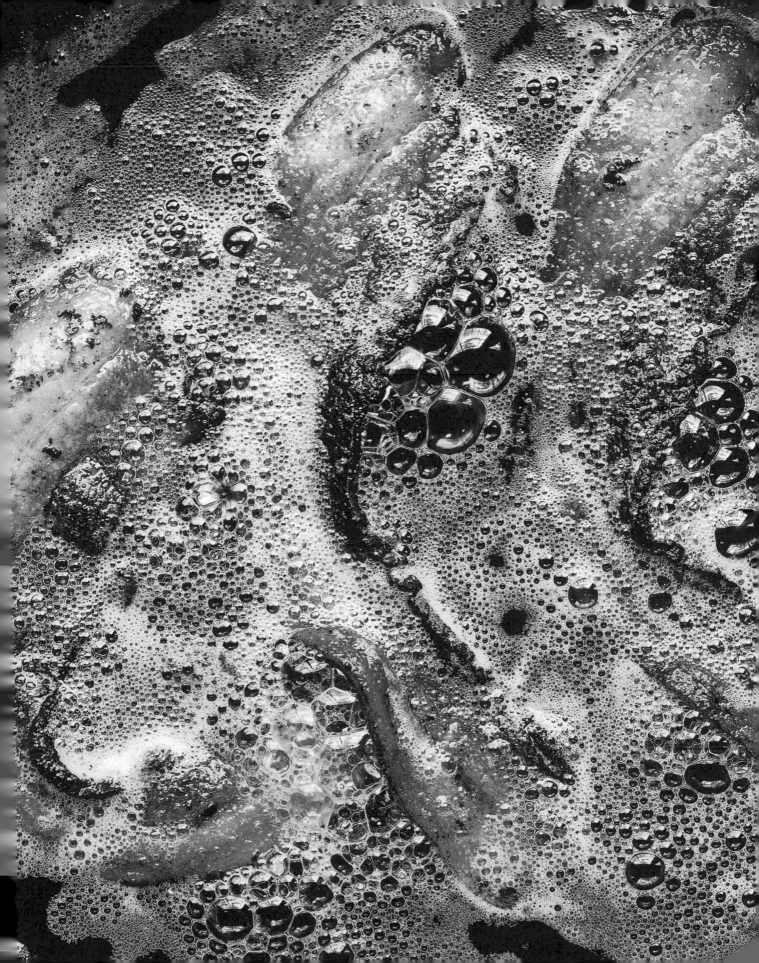

CHICKEN WINGS

YIELD: 4 servings (2 pounds of wings)

SMOKE TIME: 10 minutes

COOK TIME: 5 to 8 minutes

There's no better surprise than biting into a deep-fried hot wing and getting a hit of smoky flavor. If you're already a wing fan, this recipe is a must-try the next time you're craving wings. While you can skip the brine in this recipe if you're pressed for time, I recommend brining the wings—and really, just about all the chicken you cook. It's easy to do, and it's a guaranteed way to add flavor and keep the meat juicy during cooking.

FOR THE BRINE

- 8 cups water
- ⅓ cup kosher salt
- ⅓ cup Texas Pete hot sauce
- ¼ cup sugar
- 2 tablespoons black pepper

NOTE: Use enough of this brine to cover your wings. Store excess fresh brine in the fridge. It will keep for months if it hasn't touched any meat.

FOR THE WINGS

- 2 pounds fresh-cut chicken wings
- Peanut or canola oil, enough for deep-frying
- Buffalo Sauce (see below)

EQUIPMENT

- Large nonreactive container, such as a plastic food storage container
- Tabletop smoker
- Deep-fryer or large pot

PREPARATION

Mix together all the ingredients for the brine in a large container. This can be done ahead of time, up to a day before you smoke and fry the wings. Put the wings in the brine and place in the refrigerator for up to 3 hours. Remove the wings from the brine and rinse thoroughly.

Once you're ready to smoke, follow the Getting Started section of the tabletop smoking method on page 40. Smoke the chicken wings—working in batches so that you don't block the holes in the smoker—for 10 minutes. Remove the wings from the smoker and set aside.

Preheat your frying oil to 350°F in a deep fryer or in a pot deep enough that you don't have to worry about oil splatter. Fry the chicken wings for 5 to 8 minutes, or until golden brown and crispy, working in batches—don't crowd the fryer!

FINISHING AND SERVING

Toss the wings in the Buffalo Sauce. You can also use the wing sauce of your choice, of course, or a mixture of hot sauce and the Red Barbecue Sauce (page 26) or Mustard Sauce (page 29).

Serve immediately with blue cheese or ranch and celery or your favorite dip crudités.

BUFFALO SAUCE

- 1 cup Texas Pete (or your favorite hot sauce)
- ¼ cup cold butter, cubed
- Pinch black pepper

In a small saucepan, heat the hot sauce and slowly whisk in the cubed butter a piece or two at a time until incorporated. By working the butter in slowly, you will create an emulsion with the hot sauce. Season with pepper and refrigerate until ready to use.

SMOKY TOFU AND MUSHROOMS

YIELD: 4 servings

SMOKE TIME: 10 to 20 minutes

COOK TIME: Varies

- 1 package (16 ounces) extra-firm tofu
- ½ cup canola oil
- ½ recipe Hog Sauce (page 24)
- Juice from ½ lemon
- 1 teaspoon garlic powder
- 1 teaspoon onion powder
- Salt and pepper to taste
- 1 pound fresh mushrooms, whatever varieties you like

EQUIPMENT

- Clean kitchen towel
- Cookie sheet
- Heavy-bottomed saucepan
- Medium-size bowl
- Large resealable plastic bag
- Tabletop smoker

While this recipe outlines the basics for smoking tofu and mushrooms, I also included it to get across a big idea: you can smoke just about anything with the tabletop smoker. Even if you're not a fan of tofu, try this recipe at least once. Smoked tofu is pretty yummy and you might be surprised. As for the smoked mushrooms, while they're tasty on their own, keep in mind that they're a versatile addition to all sorts of recipes. Mushrooms already have such an interesting flavor, and smoke only increases their intensity.

PREPARATION

Wrap the tofu in a clean kitchen towel and place on a cookie sheet. Place the heavy bottomed pan on top of the tofu for 1 hour. This will press out a lot of the excess water and allow more smoke and flavor to penetrate the tofu.

Whisk the oil, Hog Sauce, lemon juice, garlic and onion powders, salt, and pepper together. Pour the liquid mixture in a large resealable plastic bag along with the pressed tofu and mushrooms. Let them marinate overnight, or for at least 5 hours.

Once you're ready to smoke, follow the Getting Started section of the tabletop smoking method on page 40. Remove the tofu and mushrooms from marinade and drain off any excess marinade. Smoke the tofu and mushrooms for 10 to 20 minutes. Remove from the smoker and set aside.

FINISHING AND SERVING

Cut the tofu and mushrooms into bite-size pieces, or adjust the size of dice to your own recipe. No matter how you cook them, though, you're going to want more surface area exposed to heat. Here are a few ideas for preparation:

- Try them sautéed in oil until golden brown. Dip or brush the fried tofu and mushrooms with any of the barbecue sauces on pages 24 to 29.
- Toss lightly in seasoned cornstarch, then deep-fry them. Serve with a dip made from soy sauce, brown sugar, and a little sesame oil, garnished with green onions.
- Use the smoked tofu and mushrooms with any recipe you like that calls for tofu or mushrooms. They will add a nice smoky flavor to the dish.

BABY BACK RIBS

YIELD: 2 servings

SMOKE TIME: 15 to 20 minutes

COOK TIME: 5 to 6 hours

- 1 fresh rack baby back ribs, about 1½ to 2 pounds
- 2 cups Rib Rub (page 30)
- Mustard Sauce or Red Barbecue Sauce (optional, pages 29 and 26)

EQUIPMENT

- Clean kitchen towel
- Large bowl
- Tabletop smoker
- Heavy-duty foil
- Wire resting rack
- Sheet pan

Baby back ribs are the most common ribs you'll find at barbecue joints—often, they're the most expensive as well. Also known as loin ribs, baby backs are cut from the rib cage between the spine and spare rib. They are typically meatier than spare ribs and are sold in racks with anywhere from eight to thirteen ribs, depending on the butcher.

Baby backs have a membrane on the underside called silverskin, which you will need to remove before smoking. If you leave it on, it will keep the rub and smoke from penetrating the meat. It also gets leathery during the cooking process. (Some ribs are sold with the silverskin removed for this reason.) If you need to remove the silverskin, it's very simple to do with just a butter knife. Dry the rib side with a clean paper towel and let it air dry for a few minutes. Run the butter knife at the edge of one of the bones near the middle of the rack. You should be able to lift a paperlike skin off of the meat. The silverskin sometimes comes off in one large sheet the size of the whole rack. If it tears or rips, just try a different part of the rack. If you find it's too slippery, try using a clean towel to grip the skin.

PREPARATION

Rinse and towel dry the baby back ribs. Place in a large bowl and generously apply the Rib Rub to both sides of the ribs, making sure to get the rub in all the nooks and crannies. Place the bowl with the ribs in the refrigerator for about 8 hours or overnight. Just like with the Boston butt, the rub almost acts like a cure and will produce a deeper, richer flavor. The salt in the rub will draw out moisture from the ribs.

Once you're ready to smoke, preheat the oven to 220°F and get your tabletop smoker going. (Follow the Getting Started section of the tabletop smoking method on page 40.) Smoke the ribs for 15 to 20 minutes. Remove the ribs from the tabletop smoker and wrap them in heavy-duty foil.

Place the ribs on a resting rack and sheet tray or a cookie tray with a fitting rack. Put the ribs in the oven and cook for 4 hours. Remove the ribs from the oven and then carefully remove the foil. Place the ribs back on the rack and pan and continue to cook for about 90 minutes or until the internal temperature is 180°F. The ribs should be tender and almost falling off the bone when they're done. Some folks like their ribs a little more toothsome while others prefer them very tender. You can adjust the cooking time (give or take 30 minutes or so) depending on your liking.

recipe continues

FINISHING AND SERVING

These baby backs are ready to go right out of the oven. If you like your ribs with just a dry rub, then enjoy them as is with baked beans, slaw, pickles, or whatever you like with your ribs! If you're a fan of saucier ribs, I would recommend the Red Barbecue Sauce (page 26) or the Mustard Sauce (page 29). If you're using a sauce, simply apply it with a brush during the last hour of oven cooking time. Apply the sauce four to five times to create a nice sweet sticky glaze and serve a little dish of the sauce on the side.

SMOKED GRITS (OR OTHER GRAINS)

YIELD: 4 to 6 servings

SMOKE TIME: 7 minutes

COOK TIME: 1½ hours

- 1 cup coarse stone-ground grits (not instant or quick-cooking)
- 4 cups water
- ¾ teaspoon salt
- 3 tablespoons unsalted butter
- 1 cup heavy cream
- ½ cup shredded extra sharp Cheddar cheese (we like Cabot)

EQUIPMENT
- Tabletop smoker

When I first tried smoking grits, I was blown away with the flavor. Once I cooked them—with lots of butter and cream—it was like eating a complete breakfast in one bite. The fat from the cream and butter and the smoky flavor tricked my mind into thinking I had added bacon!

This recipe is for grits, but use it as a template to smoke oats, wheat berries, quinoa, farro, or whatever your favorite grain may be. Try smoking rice and use it in any rice-based recipe. Play around with it. Your vegetarian friends will love you for it!

You should try to hunt down coarse stone-ground grits. You'll find the flavor is so much more complex than lower-quality grits. See if anyone is making them locally, or you can find a wide variety of heirloom grits and grains online from Anson Mills.

PREPARATION
Follow the Getting Started section of the tabletop smoking method on page 40. Place the grits on a disposable plate or a piece of aluminum foil.

Spread the layer of grits out to about ½ inch thick. Cover the smoker tightly with foil. Smoke the grits for 4 minutes. Uncover and stir the grits around, trying to get the bottom layer to the top. Cover the pan again and smoke for another 3 minutes. Uncover and set the grits aside.

Add the salt and water to a medium saucepan and bring to a boil. Whisk in the grits. Reduce the heat to a simmer and continue to whisk the grits for 20 minutes, or until the starch comes out and they thicken up. Turn off the heat and let the grits sit for 1 hour. A natural starch layer will form on top, which will trap all of the steam underneath and produce light, fluffy steamed grits. (Also, you won't get splattered with hot bubbly grits or run into the problem of having them stick to the bottom and burn!)

After an hour has passed, return the pot to a low heat and stir in the butter, heavy cream, and cheese. Cook on low for about 10 minutes.

FINISHING AND SERVING
The grits are best if served immediately, though they can be reheated in small batches with a little water added to the pot.

For leftovers, try spreading the remaining hot grits on a greased cookie sheet. Let them cool completely in the refrigerator, then cut into squares or rounds and pan fry them in a little butter. You can also smoke grits for the Grits and Gravy recipe (page 114), or add the gravy from that page to the grits recipe here if you'd like.

INFUSED SPIRITS

YIELD: One 750-milliliter bottle

- 1 cup or one large handful rinsed and cleaned spent wood chips or coals

NOTE: You will need to rinse and scrape the bigger wood chips very thoroughly. This will get off all of the ash that would otherwise cloud your spirit.

- 1 bottle (750 milliliters) rum, vodka, or the spirit of your choice

NOTE: The recipe on page 65 calls for J Wray and Nephew Overproof Jamaican Rum

EQUIPMENT

- 2 mason jars (1 quart) with lids
- Cheesecloth or other strainer

Charred wood and spirits just go together. Need proof? Look no further than bourbon, which is the spirit we love thanks to charred oak barrels. This idea was born out of that basic fact. Why not take leftover wood chips or spent chips and use them to add a smoky flavor to your favorite spirit? If you want the wood to be the primary flavor, you can try the experiment with a good-quality vodka. However, I use it to add complexity to spirits that already have been aged in wood, such as bourbon or rum.

PREPARATION

Add the wood chips or coals to the mason jar and pour the spirit over them. Close the lid and let steep for 1 month. Taste as often as you'd like. Taste it sooner than 1 month if you are concerned about the flavor developing too quickly. I've found for most wood and spirit combinations, you can let the flavors infuse for up to 2 to 3 months before they start getting a bit too strong.

Once the spirit has infused to your liking, strain it through cheesecloth or a strainer into a second mason jar.

THE TRENCHTOWN COCKTAIL

 **YIELD:** 1 cocktail

- 1 drop Scotch bonnet pepper tincture (optional)

NOTE: Soak 4 whole Scotch bonnet peppers in 250 milliliters of 100-proof vodka for 2 weeks to create this tincture.

- ¾ ounce pineapple juice, regular or smoked according to the directions that follow
- ¾ ounce wood-chip-infused J Wray and Nephew Overproof Jamaican Rum
- ¾ ounce Appleton V/X rum blend
- ½ ounce sweet vermouth
- ½ ounce lemon juice
- ⅛ ounce (1 bar spoon) St. Elizabeth Allspice Dram
- Wedge fresh pineapple, for garnish

EQUIPMENT

- Heat-proof container
- Bar spoon
- Bar shaker
- Bar strainer

This creative cocktail plays off Jamaican jerk flavors. Smoked rum is blended with regular rum and smoked pineapple juice for the base, and it gets a kick from allspice dram and a Scotch bonnet tincture.

PREPARATION

If you plan on using the Scotch bonnet tincture, you'll need to make it first, as the infusion takes a couple of weeks.

Once you have that ready, follow the Getting Started section of the tabletop smoking method on page 40 to smoke the pineapple juice. Place the pineapple juice in the smoker inside a Pyrex glass or other container that can withstand the heat. Smoke the juice for 7 minutes, or until you like the smoke level. Note that if you smoke the juice for too long, it will take on a bitter aftertaste.

Once you have all the ingredients ready, combine them into a bar shaker filled with ice. Shake the mixture until it's thoroughly mixed and chilled. Strain into a stemmed glass. Garnish with a wedge of fresh grilled pineapple.

SMOKED NUTS AND PECAN NUT BUTTER

🥄 **YIELD:** About 2 cups

🔥 **SMOKE TIME:** 5 minutes

⏱ **COOK TIME:** 10 minutes

- 2 cups pecans
- ½ teaspoon salt
- ¼ cup canola oil
- Additional salt and sugar or honey, to taste

EQUIPMENT

- Tabletop smoker
- Heavy-duty aluminum foil
- Food processor or powerful blender

Once you make pecan butter for the first time, you'll wonder why it's not something you can buy. Of course, there's one way to improve on the basic recipe: smoke the pecans first. As with homemade peanut butter, you'll find the texture is grainier than store-bought (it's similar to the "natural" peanut butter you can grind yourself in some grocery stores). As far as adding sweetener goes, it's optional, but I recommend honey or another sweet syrup if you go that route. Maple syrup, molasses, and sorghum all make for interesting variations. The same goes for the nuts. If your favorite nuts are walnuts or hazelnuts, give them a try!

PREPARATION
SMOKE THE PECANS

To smoke pecans, the first step is to remove some of the moisture. Spread the pecans on a cookie sheet and toast in the oven at 450°F for about 10 minutes. This can be done a day or more ahead of time.

To smoke the pecans, you can use the tabletop smoker or you can work them into a day at the pit. If you're smoking something large, like a pig, you'll have some downtime. Smoking nuts will kill some time and it's great for shaking up the day.

If you're using the tabletop smoker, place the pecans on a piece of foil with the edges rolled up and follow the Getting Started directions (page 40) to smoke the nuts for about 5 minutes. If you're using a pit, smoke the nuts at 200°F to 220°F for about an hour instead.

MAKE THE NUT BUTTER

Combine the smoked nuts and salt in a food processor. Process for about 5 minutes, scraping the bowl frequently, while adding the oil a little at a time. Once the oil is incorporated and the nut butter is at a consistency you like, adjust the seasoning with more salt if needed. You can also add some sugar or honey at this point.

PIT SMOKING

A WORD ON PITS

If you've only used an electric smoker, or if you've only ever had Texas-style barbecue, you probably have one idea of what smoked meat tastes like. Yet if you grew up in South Carolina or its neighboring states, you are likely used to a completely different smoky flavor in your barbecue.

The reason for these regional differences comes down to smoker design. In Texas, the most popular style of smoker utilizes a box on the side of a long pit with a draft system. The live fire draws heat through the pit, convection style, over the top of the meat and then out through the top. The smoke that surrounds the meat comes directly from hardwoods and the meat takes on a strong smoky flavor.

The Carolina style of smoking also puts the meat in direct contact with the smoke, but the hardwoods we use are often more delicate—never any mesquite—and there is no live fire. Instead, we use a separate burn barrel where wood is processed into fresh charcoal before the charcoal is loaded into the pits. The resulting meat, therefore, has a much more delicate smoky flavor. In fact, many of Buxton's out-of-state customers comment that we must "barely smoke" the meat, even though it's smoked for more than twelve hours directly over fresh charcoal! Others love the flavor of pit-smoked meats and find the Texas style over the top. That's just the way it is: regional smoking methods are different by design.

Our smokers at the restaurant are made by BQ Grills in Elm City, North Carolina. The company got its start building special rigs for barbecue competitions, but now restaurants are calling on their expertise. They still build only grills and smokers, but they have a variety of designs. The model we chose was designed by Sam Jones, the owner of Sam Jones BBQ.

The design is actually pretty simple and quite similar to the pit you can build on page 76. It's a rectangular box with a lid, doors, and a grate where the meat sits. Their design also includes rectangular pans for shoveling the coals into, which makes them easier to clean. As I mentioned though, you don't actually fire up the smoker itself.

Our process often starts at about 9 p.m., when we light the fire in our burn box (though in the busy seasons the burn box and pits are often running twenty-four hours a day). Our burn box works on the same principle as the burn barrel you'll see on page 79, but it's larger and designed with restaurant safety in mind. Anyway, we load the box with fresh local hardwood and render that down over live fire until it becomes charcoal. Once the charcoal is ready, we shovel it into one of our pits, stacking piles in the four corners. At that point the pig is already there waiting, sitting on a grate about two and a half feet above the coals.

After that, the smoking is just manual labor. We keep adding wood, making charcoal, and adding shovels of coal every twenty to thirty minutes throughout the night to keep the pit temperatures where we want them, typically between 200°F to 220°F. In this chapter, you'll find that both the small and large cinderblock pits work the same way. You'll have a separate barrel or grill where you ready your charcoal while the meat is smoked in the pit. You'll shovel coals into the pit every so often to keep it at the right temperature.

While it takes practice to control the variables and build your skill at smoking, what it doesn't take is a lot of money or any special skills. If you build a pit, even a small pit, and put in the time, you can eventually smoke meat with the best of them.

BUILDING AND USING A CINDERBLOCK PIT

To be honest, if health and safety inspectors would have let me build cinderblock pits at Buxton, I would have done it. Cement is such an ideal material for a smoker. The blocks hold in a lot of heat that escapes through sheet metal, which means you'll use less wood or coals, and the temperature will be easier to maintain throughout cooking. On the following pages, you'll find materials and instructions for a full pit that's big enough for a whole hog as well as a half-size pit. Depending on the amount of space you have at your house, I would recommend building whichever size pit you could leave for a while as a semipermanent installation. The goal is to use the pit many times before tearing it down, replacing pieces, or relocating it.

YOU WILL NEED

FULL PIT

- Measuring tape
- Shovel and hand tamp or other ground-leveling tool
- Masonry sand (optional)
- 56 cinderblocks (each 8x8x16 inches)
- 8 pieces of ½-inch rebar long enough to span the inside the pit (about 4 feet)
- Chicken wire cut to fit the inside the pit (about 7 square feet; measure your pit and then cut your chicken wire)
- Plywood or cardboard cut to cover the top of the pit
- 55-gallon drum burn barrel to feed the pit (see page 79)

HALF PIT

- Measuring tape
- Shovel and hand tamp or other ground-leveling tool
- Masonry sand (optional)
- 32 cinderblocks (each 8x8x16 inches)
- 6 pieces of ½-inch rebar long enough to span the inside of the pit (about 3 feet)
- Chicken wire cut to fit the inside the pit (about 4 square feet; measure your pit and then cut your chicken wire)
- Plywood or cardboard cut to cover the top of the pit
- Weber grill and chimney starter to feed a half-size pit (see page 79)

BUILDING A PIT

Building a pit can be an afternoon project or a full weekend's worth of work. A lot depends on the size of the pit you want to create and whether or not you want the pit to be a semipermanent installation in your yard. The longer you want the pit to last, the more precise you should be when putting it together. However, I don't recommend actually joining the blocks with any sort of cement, as some blocks will wear out sooner than others due to their exposure to fire and hot coals.

The first step is to figure out where you're going to construct your pit. You'll want level, bare earth. You don't want to build a pit on top of brush or anything else that could catch fire. And of course you'll want to keep the pit—which will have live coals and fire—away from not only your house, but also far away from any sheds and outbuildings, including decks.

For a full pit you'll be building two 4-cinderblock sides and two 3-cinderblock sides, so you'll need a clear space that's roughly 6 feet by 4½ feet. For a half-size pit, you'll build in a 2-block by 2-block configuration, so about 3 feet by 4 feet with overlap.

Measure out where the pit will go, marking the corners in the dirt. If you're not working on level dirt or if you want to add a layer of sand to aid in the leveling process, now's the time to make those adjustments. Use your shovel and tamp to create a level surface for the pit, and use masonry sand if you'd prefer. The sand can be useful for areas of land where there are a lot of little bumps in the terrain. You can use the shovel to level things off at the lowest point as best as possible, and then fill the pit base with sand. Tamping the sand will work just as well, or better, than tamping the dirt.

It may go without saying if you've ever leveled land for a home improvement project, but pay attention to the weather conditions in the days before you take on the project. You want the soil in a condition where it's easy to work with but not too soft. Depending on your drainage, usually a few days after a rain will be a good time to work. If it's winter, don't try to chisel out your pit in frozen ground!

Starting at one corner of the pit, place the first layer of blocks. Remember, two sides will have 3 blocks and two sides will have 4 blocks for the large pit—whereas it will be a 2×2 grid (though one side will be smaller where the blocks overlap) for the small pit. Once the first layer is down and everything appears level, continue to build the pit for two more layers. Once you're at the third layer, insert the pieces of rebar. Continue on and stack the fourth layer of blocks. At this point you're done with the construction of the pit.

Measure the pit and cut plywood or heavy-duty cardboard large enough to cover the entire top of your pit. I also recommend removing one vertical column of cinderblocks from the short side of your pit, as shown in the top two photos on the opposite page. You'll use this opening to add coals. Use additional plywood or even a baking sheet to cover the hole while you're smoking. Trust me, you don't want to move cinderblocks every time you add coals—plus, it will be handy to have a few extra blocks on hand for when they crack or wear out.

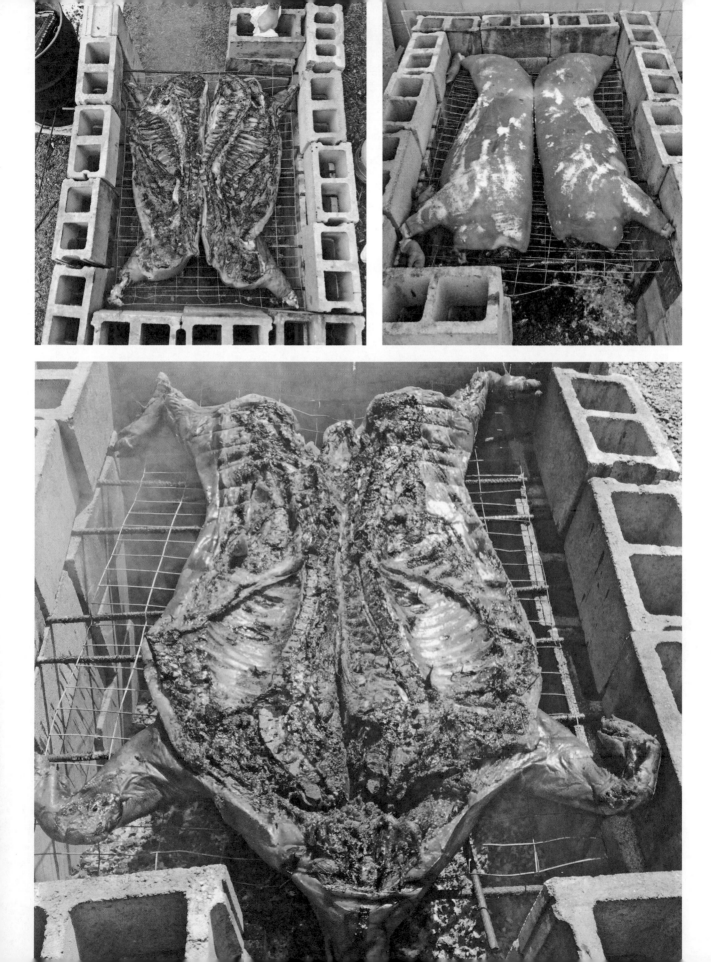

THE BURN BARREL

NOTE: As with any live fire, be careful of the sparks that are created and shoot up from the top, especially when it's windy. It can be difficult to see sparks during the day.

NOTE: As with any live fire, be careful of the sparks that are created and shoot up from the top, especially when it's windy. It can be difficult to see sparks during the day.

YOU WILL NEED

HALF PIT BURN BARREL

- Weber or other kettle-style charcoal grill
- Chimney starter

FULL PIT BURN BARREL

- 55-gallon drum or similar barrel that can withstand high temperatures and is not coated with any sort of paint or toxic coating on the interior
- Drill with ½-inch bit
- Reciprocating saw
- 5 pieces ½-inch rebar, cut to the diameter of your barrel

A burn barrel is the key to the pit. You'll find that it also becomes key to your enjoyment of the smoking process when the weather is cooler—it will keep you warm on many a cold night, and you'll find that stirring the fire soothes the soul. This is true even when you're cooking in the daytime.

BUILDING AND USING A BURN BARREL

For a small pit, a simple Weber grill and a chimney starter are all you need. To load the pit with enough charcoal to get things started, fire up the starter with charcoal. Once you're ready to transfer the charcoal to the pit, mix in a handful of the hardwood chips of your choice. This will add a bit of wood character that you'd get naturally when rendering your own charcoal with a true burn barrel.

For the larger pit, you will want to use a real burn barrel and hardwood that can be processed into charcoal. Otherwise you will be stressed out from starting loads of charcoal throughout the smoking process and you'll end up spending too much money on processed charcoal.

To create a burn barrel from your 55-gallon drum, drill two holes in the bottom to give your saw access. Then cut a hole in the side, at the bottom, that's big enough for your shovel to easily navigate inside the barrel. This is where you'll remove your charcoal once the burn barrel gets going. Drill up to twenty holes all the way around to promote airflow.

As far as the rebar goes, you can wedge it inside the burn barrel or have a local welding shop weld the rebar two-thirds of the way down. You'll want it configured so that wood rests on it while it burns and then only charcoal falls through and not large pieces of wood. It should be cross hatched with three pieces running one way and five another (see page 81).

Once the burn barrel is ready, place a sheet of cardboard on the rebar and layer split wood (about two armfuls) and shredded newspaper all the way to the top. Insert additional cardboard below the rebar and light your fire. If your wood is wet, you can use lighter fluid to help get it started.

Red and white oak are my recommended woods. You can also use some hickory and cherry, but these woods burn fast and don't make as good a charcoal. They don't burn as hot either, so you go through a lot of wood for not a lot of charcoal.

While you might have heard that you can't use wet wood for smoking, this is not the case when making charcoal. Once you have a fire going, you'll simply boil the water out of the wood quickly and the wood will process into charcoal just fine. Green wood takes longer to burn into coal, as it's wet and will take more time to dry out. However, it makes good coals. Dry wood burns fast, but the downside will be that the coals turn to ash faster.

Just don't let the fire die down or you'll have to work very hard to get it hot again.

USING THE PIT

After about 1½ hours you'll start producing charcoal. Don't mess with the fire during that time or it will mess with the integrity of your charcoal.

Remove the first shovelful of coal and transfer it to a back corner of the pit. Throw additional wood on top as the wood pile falls over the next 1½ hours. By hour three, you should have enough of the coal removed to have three shovelfuls of coal in each corner. At this point your pit will be at about 200°F to 220°F.

Using a heat-resistant thermometer, keep the pit in this range for as long as you're smoking. It's as easy—and as difficult—as continually feeding your burn barrel and adding coals to each corner as the pit temperature falls.

HALF OR WHOLE HOG

TIME: 12 hours at 220°F, or until 190°F internal temperature is reached, then 2 hours rest

TARGET INTERNAL TEMPERATURE: 190°F

COAL PLACEMENT: The 4 corners of the pit (the hog takes up most of the whole pit)

WHAT YOU NEED

- Chicken wire large enough to cover the inside of your pit (you will rest the hog on this and use it for transferring)

- One hog, approximately 180 pounds for a whole pig or 90 pounds for a half. Whole hogs should be cut down the middle so you have two half hogs for the pit.

NOTE: Smaller hogs (130 to 140 pounds) don't have enough fat, but once you get above the 180-pound range, you're going to get too much fat (and not much more meat).

RUB: Salt and pepper

SAUCE: Hog Sauce (page 24) for mixing after pulling the pork

Cooking hogs is where the dream of opening Buxton really crystallized for me. I already knew I wanted to open a barbecue restaurant, but having a gap between that initial desire and my restaurant actually opening gave me time to discover the beauty of going whole hog.

I can't remember how it started, but before I knew it, I was cooking hogs all over town. I was catering weddings, bringing the pit to local breweries' beer dinners—you name it. Over the course of many months I fell in love with the process. I would start around seven p.m., just as the sun was getting low in the sky. The sun would set and I'd work through the night, making coal by the light and warmth of the burn barrel and feeding the pit. Then, eventually, I'd see the sun rise and I knew the hog was almost ready.

I thought at Buxton I would miss those long nights under the open stars. But luckily both the timing and the restaurant itself allow me to enjoy the next best thing. I'm still often smoking hogs from sundown to sunup. And with the big windows and skylights, I can still see the sun set and rise as I work. Sometimes I turn off all the lights and pretend I'm back outside.

Okay, enough with the romance. On the pages that follow you'll find the nuts and bolts of smoking a half or whole hog. The process is nearly identical, the main difference being that half a hog is easier to move and will fit on smaller pits.

PREPARATION

SETTING UP
AND SMOKING

Because a hog smokes for 12 hours or more, you should have at least ¼ cord if not a ½ cord of wood to get through the smoking. You can also keep a couple of bags of charcoal on hand for emergency fuel. Just throw the bag of charcoal in the burn barrel and mix it with your own hot, fresh charcoal. It's a good way to get a bunch of fuel ready at once and quickly raise the temperature of a falling pit.

As far as preparing the pig goes, you should have a professional butcher cut the pig in half. From there, you can handle the rest yourself. Remove the leaf lard inside the ribcage. It should easily rip right out. Throw the leaf lard in a pot to render—you can combine that later with smoky fat from the pig, and you'll have flavored lard to use for other recipes. Around the leg, I recommend taking off the chunk of skin to give the ham more surface area while it smokes.

Next, apply salt liberally all over the surface—it's a big piece of meat, and it's hard to oversalt it. Then transfer the hog, skin side up, to the pit. I recommend putting the pig on before starting the fire in your burn barrel. The fire will take about 1½ hours to make coals, and that will give the pig time to come closer to room temperature. This way the fire doesn't have to do all the work getting the refrigerator chill off of the pig.

NOTE: As you place the hog on the pit, there's a piece of the belly you should try to flatten out, or it will fold under. More smoke will get to the inside of the hog this way, whereas if the piece were curled up you'd block some of the smoke.

Start your fire in the burn barrel and proceed to producing coals as on page 79. Cover the pit, as it can start retaining heat as soon as you start adding coals. Once the coals are ready, start making piles of coals in the pit's corners—about three shovelfuls per corner. By the time you get enough coals to load all the corners, the pit should be at about 200°F.

After that, it's all about working the coals; adding a shovelful to the piles every 20 to 30 minutes will keep the smoker at 220°F or so. Depending on your pit insulation and the weather, it could take more or less coal to keep the pit at temperature.

Once the hams and shoulders read 190°F, which takes about 12 hours, drop the pit temperature to between 180°F and 200°F and let the pig continue to cook/rest slowly as the fat melts out. You should still be adding coals, but a lot less frequently to maintain the temperature. The meat will taste better, it will be more tender, and the flesh won't be as overcooked. If it's any higher than 200°F, it will get overcooked a lot faster and you risk dried-out meat—and even starting a fire. This slow decrease in heat and rest should take about 2 hours.

NOTE: You can flip the hog over the last hour and spread the coals out to crisp the skin, but if the fire is 225°F or higher and fat renders off, you have to watch out for fires. Flipping a hog is a lot of work too. It takes two people and a lot of practice. So, in short, get a few hogs under your belt before you try this advanced maneuver.

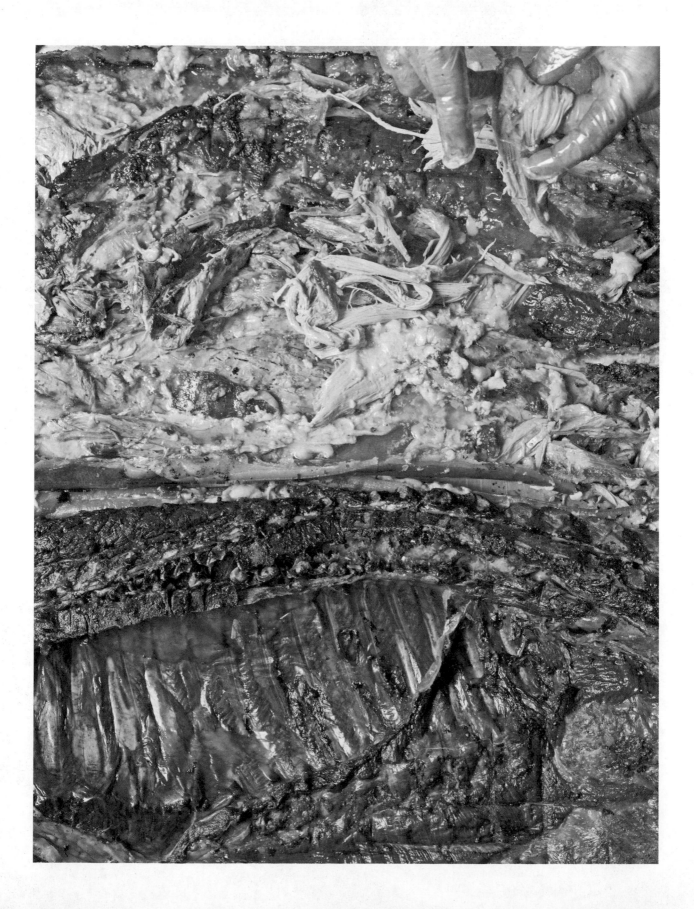

PIG PICKIN'

HERE ARE MY NOTES ON THE MEAT YOU'LL FIND:

- The belly is probably my favorite part of the pig. What you do with it depends if you want it chopped or pulled. It pretty much pulls off as a big sheet and it can pull apart almost like noodles.

- The loin is under the backbone you pulled out. If you cooked it right, you can pretty much pull that with your hands as well, though you may have to chop it.

- The tenderloin is underneath the ribs toward the ham. It's normally chopped up or pulled. It can have some bark on it as well, which you'll want to chop up—otherwise it might be too toothsome. Use the bark in other recipes, such as the collards on page 144.

- Around the shoulders the meat is pretty dark and pulls nice—lots of fat in there.

- In the ham there are a lot of muscles that can pull really nice, but typically people chop the ham as it's the hardest part to cook right. It's a thick piece of meat with a lot of muscle.

Once the pig is done, it will take two to three people with gloves on to pick up the pig by the chicken wire and bring it to the table where you plan to process it. At the restaurant, we do the same thing as you would at home. We carry it on the chicken wire and flip it over onto the table so that the skin side is down. Let it sit for thirty to forty minutes to give the juices time to seep back into the meat. If you pull the pig right away, you'll lose a lot of the fat and flavor.

Once the pig has rested, start the picking by removing the spine and the ribs (see the photo on page 86). for a visual of this and the steps that follow). Unfortunately, the spine and ribs won't come out in one piece. The silverskin is attached to the ribs though, so you may have some luck getting many of the ribs out together. You will still want to try to pull the rib meat off the silverskin. The silverskin itself is one of the few parts of the pig you can just get rid of. There's also a shoulder bone or blade, which should be removed next—it's what you find in Boston butts—and a piece of cartilage that's often separate. Then there's the leg bone you will have to pull out. To finish removing the bones, take out the hip socket bones from the ham, the leg bones, and trotter bones.

Once you've chopped or pulled all the meat, season it all with a nice dusting of salt, and use about $2/3$ gallon of Hog Sauce for a whole pig. I recommend mixing it all together inside the skin. You can do it on a cutting board if you prefer, but the meat can get cold too quickly. Mixing inside the skin helps the layer of fat get mixed in, and the meat stays hot. However, you will want to remove any large pieces of fat, typically found under the meat and attached to the skin.

NOTE: The meat and especially the fat will burn your hands even after an hour of being out of the pit. Even with gloves on, pork fat feels hot for a long time!

What I've found with whole hog is that the fat and the vinegar will emulsify as it coats the meat, almost like a dressing. Once you cool it down, you'll see the fat and, reheated, it can break down and seem oilier.

You don't have to finish a whole pig at once, but it's a good idea to have some friends ready because the meat is always best when you eat it right away! While you can use it in various recipes or top it with various sauces, I prefer it straight-up, piled on soft white bread.

ST. LOUIS RIBS OR SPARERIBS

TIME: 5 hours at 200°F to 220°F, though they can go a little longer

TARGET INTERNAL TEMPERATURE: 180°F is when the fat melts, but I look for when the bone starts to pull apart from the meat as the definitive sign that the ribs are done

COAL PLACEMENT: Mostly direct

YIELD: 1 rack of ribs (about 2 servings)

MEAT: 1 rack spareribs (about 1¼ pounds per rack)

RUB: Rib Rub (page 30)

BASTE: Hog Sauce (page 24) about halfway through

SAUCE: Red Barbecue Sauce (page 26) last 30 minutes

In some people's eyes, spareribs are less appealing than baby backs. Many also say they're harder to cook. I've never agreed with either of those sentiments. Especially as the cost for baby backs nears twice that of spareribs, I wonder why more people aren't cooking them. Beyond the value, though, I find that spareribs have more flavor and often a bit more fat than baby backs—making them more forgiving to cook. The extra fat, of course, also helps add additional flavor. St. Louis ribs are just a special cut of spareribs that save you from having to deal with the full sparerib cartilage. If you've ever seen "rib tips," that's the matching piece cut off a full sparerib when making the St. Louis cut.

PREPARATION

Rub the ribs with the Rib Rub right before you put them on the smoker; a little bit prior is okay. Rib Rub is mostly brown sugar, so definitely monitor these ribs as you smoke them. Move them off to the side if there's a hotspot. Let the hotspot die down and then move them back. I also recommend flipping them and basting them with Hog Sauce throughout the cooking process to give them some acid.

During the last 30 minutes, as the ribs approach the finish line, start basting them with the Red Barbecue Sauce or your own favorite rib sauce. If you start

basting any earlier, the extra sugar will start to burn. Going a full hour will definitely put some char on your sauce.

Remove them after 5 hours, or when the meat starts pulling away from the bone. I like them on the early side of done, where the meat is still kind of attached to the bone and they have some chew to them. Basically, if you push between ribs and your fingers start to go through the meat, they're done. If the meat is still too firm, cook longer. If you want even more tender, falling-off-the-bone ribs, wrap them in foil and let them continue to smoke for an additional 1 to 2 hours.

PIT BEEF

⏱ **TIME:** 2 to 3 hours at 200°F to 220°F, or 3 to 5 hours at 180°F to 200°F (go by internal temperature as beef cuts vary so much in thickness)

🌡 **TARGET INTERNAL TEMPERATURE:** 125°F for medium rare

🪨 **COAL PLACEMENT:** Direct

🍴 **YIELD:** 10 to 12 servings

WHAT YOU NEED

MEAT: 4 to 5 pounds top round

RUB: ½ cup ground coffee mixed with ½ cup ground pepper

BRINE: Beef Brine (page 100)

SAUCE: Pit Beef Sauce (page 93)

While everyone knows us for whole-hog barbecue, that doesn't mean that people weren't asking for beef from day one. While a lot of barbecue places end up specializing in brisket, we went down a different path. We imagined what it would be like if you went back in time and got one of the first sandwiches at that iconic fast-food restaurant famous for thinly sliced roast beef.

As for the cut, our Pit Beef is top round, though we trim it to clean up some of the fat. And because some pieces are bigger and some are smaller, this is one of the few meats where we really need to go by internal temperature. If your cut has any "flappy" pieces, tie them up with butcher's twine to get a more uniform, even shape for your roast, which will make it easier to handle and cook evenly.

PREPARATION

Brine the beef overnight just before you smoke it. On smoking day, rub it until it's heavily coated with the black pepper and coffee.

Now, keep in mind that you're basically making roast beef in a smoker. This means you'll need to pay close attention if you want it to be a perfect medium rare. Smoke the meat at about 200°F until the meat reaches 125°F internally. It depends on the size of your roast and how well you hold temperature, but it will be somewhere in between 2 and 4 hours. If you have the patience, you can add additional smoke flavor by smoking the beef at a lower temperature. By lowering the smoker to 180°F or so, you can add an additional hour or two of smoking time.

Once the beef reaches temperature, pull it off, let it rest, then slice thin and serve. If you're not eating it right away or saving it for the leftovers, refrigerate the beef. You'll find this also makes it easier to slice very thin, if that's your thing.

If you want to recreate the Buxton sandwich and you're using cold sliced beef, use a sauté pan to heat up the beef and coat it with as much or as little of the Pit Beef Sauce as you'd like. Serve on a pan-toasted white roll with Horseradish Sauce on one side.

HORSERADISH SAUCE

- ½ cup sour cream
- ½ cup mayonnaise (preferably Duke's)
- ½ cup prepared horseradish
- 1 tablespoon ground black pepper
- 3 cloves garlic, crushed
- Juice of 1 lemon
- Pinch of salt
- Handful of chopped parsley

Combine all ingredients in a small mixing bowl and stir well to combine. Cover and store in the fridge for up to 1 week.

PIT BEEF SAUCE

- 3 cups ketchup
- ½ cup water
- ½ cup Hog Sauce (page 24)
- 1 cup Hog Stock (page 32)
- ¼ cup Worcestershire sauce
- 1 teaspoon garlic powder
- 1 teaspoon onion powder
- 1 teaspoon ground black pepper
- Pinch of hickory smoke powder

Combine all the ingredients in a medium saucepan. Bring to a simmer and cook for 15 minutes. Mop over the pit beef toward the end of cooking or when serving. This sauce can be made ahead of time and stored up to a week in the fridge.

SMOKED CHICKEN

⏱ **TIME:** 2 to 3 hours at 200°F to 220°F

🌡 **TARGET INTERNAL TEMPERATURE:** 155°F

COAL PLACEMENT: Direct

YIELD: 2 to 4 servings (depending on the chicken size)

YOU WILL NEED

MEAT: 1 chicken (2 to 3 pounds)

BRINE: Chicken Brine (page 124)

SAUCE: Red Barbecue Sauce (page 26) and a bit of hog fat or butter

My granddad's welding business in Florence, South Carolina, used to make grills and other cookers. On Fridays he'd barbecue some chickens, and it seemed like the whole town would stop by. You'd see the politicians and policemen eating chicken and drinking beer every week at that shop. Eventually my dad took over cooking the chickens, and growing up we certainly ate more barbecue chicken than pork.

At Buxton, I think it's important for us to try to sell out of the chicken the same day we make it. At home, you'll find that it keeps just fine overnight, but there's nothing quite like fresh out of the pit—that's when this chicken is at its best.

PREPARATION

First, brine your chicken for 5 hours or overnight. Once the chicken is brined, pat the chicken dry and sprinkle with a little black pepper.

Before you place the chicken on the smoker, either spatchcock it or break it in half. I actually think halves work better. They're easier to move. Don't go any further than this—a quartered chicken will lose moisture and cook less evenly. Place it on the smoker bone side down, skin side up. If you're smoking a lot of meat in one day, it's fine to lay the chickens around a pig or alongside other meat.

Cook the chicken 2 to 3 hours with the pit at 200°F to 220°F. About halfway through cooking, dunk the chicken in the red sauce and from that point forward baste it a few times as it finishes cooking.

While the food safety guidelines say 165°F, I recommend taking chicken off the smoker once it hits 155°F. It will continue to cook after you take it off the smoker, and I don't know that I've ever had chicken cooked to 165°F that wasn't dry. There might be pink on the bone, but I've been eating chicken that way a long time. And when I'm cooking out, I would rather have one person think they're not eating something that's safe than serve everyone dried chicken! That said, if you get busy, chicken can hang out a little longer on the smoker without getting too dry.

At serving time, it's great if the skin is a little crispy. You may need to throw it on a gas or charcoal grill or flip it over on the smoker above some fresh coals to crisp it up. You can also broil it just before serving.

PULLED TURKEY

TIME: 5 hours at 200°F to 220°F

TARGET INTERNAL TEMPERATURE: 165°F

COAL PLACEMENT: Direct

YIELD: About 12 servings

YOU WILL NEED

MEAT: 1 turkey (16 to 18 pounds)

BRINE: Turkey Brine (below)

BASTE: Hog Sauce (page 24)

Smoking a whole turkey can be fun at Thanksgiving, but I'll let you in on a secret: smoking a turkey and pulling it like pork is delicious year-round. Some of the barbecue restaurants in South Carolina are in on the secret, but I haven't seen it served in very many places. I don't know the origins, but it might be to provide a pulled meat for the customers who don't eat pork. Of course, this also makes a great shareable main dish around the holidays when everyone wants turkey. The white meat and dark meat are all mixed up with the turkey fat and sauce, and nobody has to fight over the drumstick.

PREPARATION

First, brine your turkey for at least 8 hours or overnight. Once the turkey is brined, pat it dry.

I spatchcock the turkey before placing it on the smoker, skin side up. This helps it cook more evenly and absorb more smoke flavor.

Cook the turkey for 4 hours with the pit at 200°F to 220°F. At this point, flip it over and punch holes through the meat behind the ribs, making little crevices. Baste the rib section heavily with the Hog Sauce, making sure it pools in the crevices. This will help the breast meat stay moist.

I recommend taking turkey off the smoker once it approaches or hits 165°F in most places, with the breast at 160°F.

Remove the meat from the bones, and discard or save the skin for other purposes. Be careful with the small leg bones of the turkey—they can slip through and you don't want them in with the meat. At Buxton we pull it with our hands and it shreds apart like pulled pork. If you prefer a more chopped style of barbecue, feel free to use a knife as well.

You can serve it on a sandwich as is or toss it with additional Hog Sauce.

TURKEY BRINE

- 2 gallons sweet tea
- 2 cups Texas Pete hot sauce
- 1 cup salt
- ¼ cup fennel seed
- ¼ cup ground black pepper
- 3 dried bay leaves
- 1 bunch thyme

Whisk all ingredients together well, until salt has combined with the rest of the brine. You can make this brine a few days ahead of time and store it in the fridge.

TURKEY BREAST RUBBED WITH HERBS

TIME: 2 to 3 hours at 200°F to 220°F

TARGET INTERNAL TEMPERATURE: 165°F

COAL PLACEMENT: Indirect or direct

YIELD: 6 servings

YOU WILL NEED

MEAT: 1 turkey breast (about 4 pounds)

BRINE: Turkey Brine (page 96)

RUB: ¼ cup ground fennel seed, ¼ cup black pepper, and ¼ cup herbes de Provence

You might think this turkey breast would turn out similar to the Pulled Turkey, but it actually tastes quite a bit different. It came about as we tried to envision a new turkey sandwich for the menu. To create an open-faced turkey sandwich, we ended up treating it more like Pit Beef than whole turkey: the breast is smoked similar to a roast and then sliced thin like deli meat. One day, we plan on having a full deli case at Buxton. But for now this turkey comes and goes as an open-faced turkey sandwich special, topped with Hog Gravy.

PREPARATION

Brine the breast for 12 hours.

Once you're ready to smoke, pat the breast dry and coat it with rub.

Cook it for 2 to 3 hours at 200°F to 220°F, flipping once halfway through cooking. You'll find the brined breast is pretty forgiving and you really don't have to do much. Basically, the only thing you'd have to worry about is if you have it directly over coals when the coals are very hot. You can still smoke it this way, but it will cook faster and you'll have to monitor it more closely to make sure it doesn't dry out.

The sandwich we make is an open-faced sandwich, with turkey meat stacked high on a griddled bun with smoked cheddar and smoked Gouda cheese. Both sides are then topped with Hog Gravy (page 114). If you want to go a step further, add a dollop of apple chutney for a fruity contrast.

BEEF SHORT RIBS

TIME: 8 to 10 hours

TARGET INTERNAL TEMPERATURE: 200°F

COAL PLACEMENT: Indirect

YIELD: 3 to 4 servings

YOU WILL NEED

MEAT: 1 rack short ribs (3 to 5 pounds)

RUB: ½ cup black pepper and ½ cup ground coffee

BRINE: Beef Brine (see below)

SAUCE: Hog Sauce (page 24) and Red Barbecue Sauce (page 26)

Back before I owned a barbecue restaurant, while working in fine dining, I played around with short ribs quite a bit. It used to be one of those secretly good cuts: it was inexpensive—for rib meat—but the flavor was so good when you treated the meat right. Like a nice piece of roast beef, beef ribs are just succulent. In those days, I used to quick-smoke them using a method like that on page 40 and then braise them. But at Buxton, we smoke them from start to finish, of course. As for the rub, I took inspiration from Texas-style barbecue, which seems to hardly ever use any sugar on beef.

PREPARATION

Brine the ribs overnight.

When you're ready to smoke the ribs, rub them heavily with the black pepper and coffee. A lot of it will fall off, but what sticks will be flavorful enough.

Unlike the St. Louis Spareribs (page 90) there's no sugar in this rib rub. That means these ribs don't have to be monitored quite as closely and you can have a relatively easy day smoking them. During the last 3 hours, you should notice the ribs becoming softer and jiggly to the touch.

When they're done, between hours 8 and 10, they should read 200°F internally. Basically, if you push between ribs and your fingers start to go through the meat, it's done. If it still is too firm, cook a bit longer. As with spareribs, I like them on the early side of done, where the meat is still kind of attached to the bone and they have some chew to them. But if you like fall-off-the-bone ribs, cover them with foil and cook them 1 to 2 hours longer.

Take the ribs off the smoker, baste them with Hog Sauce, and let them rest for 30 minutes. I like to serve them with Red Barbecue Sauce, but the Mustard Sauce goes well with them too.

BEEF BRINE

- 8 cups water
- ¼ cup kosher salt
- ½ cup granulated sugar
- 1½ teaspoons pickling spice
- ¼ cup packed dark brown sugar
- 2 tablespoons honey
- 3 garlic cloves, minced
- 1½ teaspoons coriander seed
- 1½ teaspoons black peppercorn

Combine all ingredients in a large container.

EIGHTEENTH-CENTURY BARBECUE LAMB

TIME: 3 to 4 hours at 200°F to 220°F, or 4 to 7 hours at 180°F to 200°F

TARGET INTERNAL TEMPERATURE: 130°F to 140°F

COAL PLACEMENT: Direct

YIELD: Serves 12 to 15 people

YOU WILL NEED

MEAT: 1 lamb shoulder (about 6½ pounds)

RUB: Salt and pepper

SAUCE: Eighteenth-Century North Carolina Barbecue Sauce (page 103)

Craig Rodgers is the owner of Border Springs Farm in Virginia. If you've never heard of Craig, trust me when I say he's a big deal in the lamb business. He used to deliver or ship his lambs on his own. And even though he now partners with a few select companies, he is still well known for his quality lamb.

Anyway, I was lucky enough to have Craig stop in at Buxton one day shortly after we opened. He told me I should try barbecuing lamb—after all, Americans had been barbecuing it since the days of the founding fathers. This caught my attention, and it turns out that Thomas Jefferson did indeed barbecue lamb. Inspired by history, I looked back to early (eighteenth-century) North Carolina barbecue sauces for this recipe. You'll notice a big difference from today's sauces when it comes to the seasonings as well as the acid: they used lemon juice instead of vinegar.

PREPARATION

When your smoker is ready, rub the lamb with salt and pepper.

For the lamb, your goal is to smoke it to medium, which is 130°F to 140°F internal. This should take between 2 and 4 hours at 200°F to 220°F depending on how consistent you keep the smoker temperature and the lamb's location in the pit. Just like the Pit Beef, if you want additional smoke flavor on the lamb, instead of smoking at 200°F to 220°F, you can smoke at a lower temperature, like 180°F. This will let you smoke the lamb for additional hours as it reaches temperature and it will continue to absorb smoky flavor.

Once the lamb reaches temperature, pull it off and let it rest. After it's rested for 15 minutes, it's ready to serve. The way we like to prepare it at Buxton is to roughly chop it into cubes while still warm and then transfer it to a sauté pan where some of the barbecue sauce is already warming. You just want to use the pan like a warm mixing bowl—you don't want to cook the lamb any further.

Serve the warm lamb on a sandwich or as a holiday main dish with sides such as dressing, potatoes, and vegetables.

Note that instead of chopping the whole lamb, you can also refrigerate it and slice it thin like deli meat for sandwiches.

EIGHTEENTH-CENTURY NORTH CAROLINA BARBECUE SAUCE

- 1 750-milliliter bottle of your favorite white wine

NOTE: Keep in mind the sweetness of the wine will affect the sweetness of the sauce.

- ¼ cup rubbed sage
- Juice of 2 lemons

- 2 tablespoons crushed red pepper
- 2 tablespoons chopped garlic
- 2 tablespoons ground black pepper
- ¼ cup sugar

In a medium saucepan, bring the wine to a boil over medium heat. If you're working on a gas stove, be careful, as alcohol can catch on fire as it burns out. Once the alcohol has cooked out, about 10 minutes, add the remaining ingredients and reduce the heat to a simmer. Cook for 5 minutes, then remove from the heat and let cool. The sauce is ready to use immediately and will keep 1 to 2 weeks in the fridge.

EMBERED VEGETABLES

YOU WILL NEED

- Any vegetables you want to smoke
- Cast-iron pan or hotel pan (page 40)

All over the country, restaurants are adding live fires and coal-burning ovens to their kitchens. At Buxton, it was less about tapping into this trend and more about making the most of the pits we already had going. If we're going to spend that much money on wood, why not use it to cook everything we can?

The same can be said of a home pit. It takes a lot of time—and wood—to keep one going for any length of time. So start thinking of pit days with an open mind. Have a bag of onions? Throw them in the pit! Thinking of making salsa later in the week? Roast those tomatoes and peppers. Even when it comes to something as simple as potatoes, smoke 'em if you got 'em.

MY ADVICE FOR SMOKING VEGETABLES

- If you're planning on cooking something from start to finish, add the vegetables with at least 3 hours of pit time left.

- Use a cast-iron pan or hotel pan for your vegetables unless you really want to bury them in the embers. While the photo at left looks pretty dreamy, the reality is that putting your vegetables in the coals can make them harder to remove, and they will be covered in ash. Keeping them in a pan will let you easily move them in and out of the pit and keep most of the ash off of them.

- If you have meat cooking above the vegetables and it's dripping fat, place the vegetables below to catch some of the fat. It will enhance the flavor of your vegetables, at the least. At best, it could be that a flavorful vegetable like brussels sprouts can be served straight from the pit, simply dressed with salt and pepper.

HERE ARE A FEW FAVORITES

CARROTS, ONIONS, AND BEETS
I am constantly throwing these in the pit. For onions in particular, a pit onion can replace a regular onion and add complexity to many recipes. And because onions have skin, you can throw them right on the coals if you'd like; you'll be peeling them later anyway.

POTATOES
I recommend cutting up potatoes and placing them in a cast-iron pan. Cutting them up will increase their surface area, and they will cook more quickly.

CORN
Corn is wonderful with smoky flavor, both on its own and in dishes like the Embered Creamed Corn on page 161.

PEPPERS
Green, red, and spicy peppers are a great fit for the pit.

TOMATOES AND OTHER DELICATE VEGETABLES
These can have a tendency to explode if they get too hot, so keep them away from coals or add them as the pit starts to die down for the day.

BRUSSELS SPROUTS AND CABBAGE
As I mention on page 22, we smoke our brussels sprouts in our pit in a pan underneath the hogs. It doesn't get much better than that.

BUXTON FAVORITES

Catfish Stew

Chicken Bog

Grits and Gravy

Barbecue Hash

Cured, Smoked, and Fried Catfish

Hush Puppies

Tartar Sauce

Fried Chicken Sandwich

Smoked Pimento Cheese

Pimento Cheese Ball

Fermented Chow-Chow

Christmas Quiche

Smoked Deviled Eggs

CATFISH STEW

YIELD: 8 servings, about 1 cup each

- 3 slices bacon, diced

NOTE: We use our own house bacon. If you buy bacon, make sure to buy high-quality smoked bacon, such as Nueske's, or smoke it yourself first.

- 3 stalks celery, diced
- 1 medium carrot, diced
- 1 medium onion, diced
- 1 clove garlic, minced
- 2 cans (28 ounces each) crushed whole tomatoes
- ¼ cup Worcestershire sauce
- ¼ cup Texas Pete hot sauce
- 1 tablespoon paprika
- ¼ teaspoon celery seed
- 1 dried bay leaf
- 1½ cups water
- Sugar to taste
- 2-pound catfish filet, cut into 1-inch pieces
- Salt and pepper to taste
- Steamed cooked rice, for serving (optional)

Buxton Hall is a large restaurant, so when I say that my granddad, R.T. Moss, had a pond in his backyard the size of our place—well, that's a good-size catfish pond. On Sundays, my family used to go over there to fish and my granddad would usually cook lunch for us afterward. He'd fry up the fish sometimes, but most of the time he'd make his catfish stew.

His was a stewed tomato-based style; he'd even use the tomatoes that my grandma had put up if they were on the shelf. I've reimagined it a bit to create our Catfish Stew at Buxton, but the secret to both soups is the same: add some of the catfish toward the beginning instead of adding it all at the end. The early addition of catfish will break down and infuse the whole stew with catfish flavor. (Of course, it's also a good way to utilize the scraps after you cut the chunks for the stew.)

PREPARATION

Fry the bacon in a large pot over medium heat until the fat renders off and the meat gets nice and crisp. Add the celery, carrot, onion, and garlic; continue to cook until the vegetables soften, about 5 to 10 minutes. Add the crushed tomatoes, Worcestershire, Texas Pete, paprika, celery seed, bay leaf, and water. You can also add a little sugar, to taste.

Bring the mixture to a simmer. Now's the time where you should add some of the catfish scraps and maybe a few of the larger chunks. Then cover the pot and simmer for about 40 minutes, or until the catfish and vegetables are tender.

At this point, go ahead and add the rest of the catfish. Continue to cook uncovered for 10 to 15 minutes, or until the fish is cooked through and flaky. Discard the bay leaf; add salt and pepper to taste.

Serve over a bowl of steamed rice or on its own with a few saltine crackers on the side. If you'd like to spice it up, add a few drops of Texas Pete sauce on top.

CHICKEN BOG

🥄 **YIELD:** About 8 servings as a main dish, more as a side

FOR THE CHICKEN BOG STOCK

- 1 whole chicken, about 1½ pounds
- ½ cup whole black peppercorns
- ½ head celery, chopped
- 1½ pounds carrots, chopped
- ½ bunch fresh thyme
- ½ teaspoon crushed red pepper
- ¼ cup smoked hog fat or ¼ cup (½ stick) butter
- 9 cups water

FOR THE CHICKEN BOG

- 8 cups chicken bog stock
- Chicken meat from the stock recipe above
- 4 cups uncooked long-grain rice
- 1 pound smoked pork sausage (like kielbasa), sliced
- ¼ cup freshly ground black pepper
- 2 cups frozen peas
- Salt to taste

I love Chicken Bog because it's one of those very regional recipes that has survived for generations in just a few specific places. In the case of Chicken Bog, the recipe comes from the Pee Dee region of South Carolina. It's a gumbolike dish that combines homemade chicken stock and sausage with rice and peas. If you've ever been to Charleston, you might have tried a similar dish under the name "purloo" or "chicken rice."

The chicken bog my grandparents used to make is the basis for our bog at Buxton. It's a Florence and Myrtle Beach version of bog that was passed down to my mom and then to me. While it's a simple and humble dish, a good bog is built on the homemade, slow-cooked chicken and stock. So don't take any shortcuts with this recipe.

PREPARATION

MAKE THE STOCK

Place the chicken, peppercorns, celery, carrots, thyme, crushed pepper, and fat in a large stock pot and cover with the water. Bring to a boil and simmer until the chicken is cooked through, about 30 minutes. Remove the chicken and set aside. Strain the stock through a fine mesh strainer into a large bowl or container. Don't skim or otherwise remove the fat from the stock though—it will help flavor the bog.

Let the chicken cool and then pick the meat, setting it aside for the bog recipe that follows. The broth will store for up to a week in the fridge, but as you're using the meat for the bog, I'd recommend making the bog within a 1 to 2 days.

MAKE THE CHICKEN BOG

Bring the chicken stock to a boil in a large pot with a tight-fitting lid. Add the chicken you set aside when making the stock, rice, sausage, and black pepper. Bring back to a boil and taste for seasoning. You might want to add a bit of salt at this point.

Reduce to a simmer, cover with the lid, and cook on low for 20 minutes, stirring once or twice in the first 5 minutes and then leaving the lid on. Turn off the heat and let it sit for 10 minutes. Remove the lid, add the peas, and stir up everything.

Serve immediately. I like garnishing with Texas Pete hot sauce.

GRITS AND GRAVY

YIELD: 6 servings, about 1 cup each

FOR THE HOG GRAVY

- ½ cup (1 stick) butter
- 1 cup all-purpose flour
- 2 cups milk
- 2 cups Hog Stock (page 32) or the stock of your choice
- 2½ cups buttermilk
- Pinch garlic powder
- Pinch onion powder
- Salt and pepper to taste
- 2 tablespoons Texas Pete hot sauce

FOR THE GRITS

- 4 cups water
- 1 cup milk
- 1 cup grits
- ½ cup buttermilk
- 2 jalapeño peppers, finely diced
- 2 ears corn, shucked and kernels cut off cob
- ½ cup goat cheese
- 1 tablespoon butter
- Salt and pepper to taste
- Popped popcorn, as desired, for serving

Like children all over the south, I ate my fair share of grits growing up. That's probably why as I trained to become a chef, I found myself drawn to grits from the start. I still remember myself as a young chef, trying to impress my wife-to-be on one of our early dates with a "fancy" meal of shrimp and grits.

I'm clearly not the only Southern chef in love with grits. You'll now find slow-cooked Anson Mills grits on many menus across the region—and beyond. Here in Asheville though, we're lucky to have Dave Bauer, the owner of Farm and Sparrow. Dave mills our grits from a local variety of corn called PJ White, and he mills them nice and coarse. The screen he uses to pass them through originally had a hole in it, and I liked the super-coarse texture so much that he still uses that screen just for us. The message here, though, is to source your grits as locally as you can, or order the highest-quality grits you can find if you want to make the best bowl.

PREPARATION

MAKE THE HOG GRAVY

In a medium saucepan, melt the butter over medium heat and add the flour, stirring continually with a whisk and cooking until the mixture is light brown. (It should smell like fresh popcorn.)

Add the milk, hog stock, and buttermilk. Bring to a boil while stirring frequently and then reduce to a simmer. Add the garlic powder, onion powder, salt, and pepper. Cook over low heat for 5 minutes. Adjust seasoning and finish with Texas Pete.

This gravy can be served immediately or refrigerated for 5 days.

MAKE THE GRITS

It's important to note that our grits haven't been treated to be quick-cooking grits. While most people cook grits like this for an hour, stirring constantly, I find that they turn out even better with a longer cooking period but a shorter active cooking time. In other words, they still take quite a while, but you don't have to stir them for an hour, which is nice.

Start by bringing the water and milk to a boil in a large pot with a tight-fitting lid. Stir in the grits and adjust the heat until bubbles slowly come to the surface. Cook the grits, stirring frequently, for 10 to 20 minutes, or until the starch comes out and they thicken up.

Now cut the heat and stop stirring. You'll see that the starch makes a filmy top layer—almost like you put a layer of plastic wrap on the grits. The layer of starch keeps a lot of the heat and steam underneath, and the grits will slowly continue to cook. Leave them alone for about an hour.

After the hour is up, turn the heat back on low to medium-low and add the buttermilk, jalapeños, corn, cheese, and butter. Cook for about 15 to 20 minutes. Adjust seasoning with salt and pepper to taste. Serve with a ladle of the gravy and a few pieces of popcorn, if desired.

BARBECUE HASH

YIELD: 6 servings, about 1 cup each

- 1 pound leftover pulled pork or whole-hog barbecue
- ½ pound chicken liver, finely chopped or ground
- 1 medium onion, finely diced or ground
- 1 or 2 cloves garlic, finely diced
- 1 tablespoon kosher salt
- 1 tablespoon freshly ground black pepper
- ½ tablespoon onion powder
- ½ tablespoon garlic powder
- 2 cups Red Barbecue Sauce (page 26)
- 1 cup Mustard Sauce (page 29)
- 8 cups water, divided
- ¼ cup Worcestershire sauce
- 2 tablespoons Texas Pete hot sauce
- 1 cup cooked white rice
- Additional hot white rice, for serving

Like Chicken Bog, Barbecue Hash is a regional dish from South Carolina that I fell in love with. No doubt, there are as many varieties of hash as there are barbecue restaurants. The style we make at Buxton falls into the midlands style—if there is such a thing. The recipe that follows is our base recipe, but feel free to play around with it to make your own house hash. Substitute leftover smoked chicken for leftover pulled pork. Try it with potatoes instead of rice. You get the idea: there's no wrong way to make a hash.

PREPARATION

Add the pork, chicken liver, onion, and garlic to a large pot. Season them with the salt, pepper, and onion and garlic powders. Cook over medium heat until the meat is slightly browned. Add both barbecue sauces, 5 cups of water, Worcestershire, Texas Pete, and 1 cup cooked rice. Bring to a boil, then reduce the heat to low so that the mixture is at a simmer.

Cook at a simmer for about 1½ hours, uncovered, stirring frequently to avoid sticking. Add about 2 cups of water and continue to cook and stir for another 1½ hours. Add a final cup of water and cook for 45 minutes or until the water has reduced to leave you with a loose, meaty, gravylike consistency.

Serve over hot white rice. Garnish with additional hot sauce and soda crackers.

CURED, SMOKED, AND FRIED CATFISH

YIELD: 5 servings

FOR THE CURE

- 1 cup kosher salt
- 1 cup sugar
- 1 tablespoon celery seed
- 2 dried bay leaves

- 5 catfish fillets, 5 to 7 ounces each

When I was growing up, I often spent afternoons with my dad at his welding shop, which was in an industrial part of town. There was only one place to eat down there, a little hole-in-the-wall cafe that served seafood. It was one of those places where you could pop in just to buy fresh fish, or you could buy a fish and they'd fry it up for you in back with some hush puppies.

At Buxton, I was inspired by the goodness of those memories. It's hard to beat perfectly fried fresh catfish. However, we wanted to add a bit of smoke to our catfish before we fried it. It turns out, that isn't as easy as it sounds: catfish is delicate and you can quickly overcook it. Eventually, though, we figured it out. We now cure the catfish with a salt and sugar mix before we smoke it. This lets us smoke the fish for just long enough to pick up a delicate smoke flavor before we fry it without taking a turn for the worse in consistency. If you're making this recipe at home, Hush Puppies (page 121) are optional—but if you're firing up the fryer anyway, I highly recommend making them.

PREPARATION

MAKE THE CURE

The catfish needs to cure before any of the other steps, so make the cure mixture first. Process the salt, sugar, celery seed, and bay leaves in a food processor or small blender until the bay leaves and celery seed are finely ground. Coat your catfish fillets and let them cure at room temperature for about 30 minutes.

recipe continues

FOR THE CATFISH DREDGE

- 2 cups cornmeal
- 1 tablespoon plus 1 teaspoon ground black pepper
- 1 tablespoon onion powder
- 1 tablespoon garlic powder
- 1 tablespoon paprika
- 1 tablespoon salt
- 1 tablespoon cornstarch

FOR THE CATFISH MOP
(OPTIONAL)

- ¾ cups Hog Sauce (page 24)
- 10 ounces ketchup

FOR FRYING

- Canola oil (enough to fill your deep fryer or enough to cover the catfish halfway in a cast iron pan)
- 1 cup all-purpose flour
- Egg wash (1 cup of buttermilk whisked together with 1 egg)

FOR SERVING

- Lemon wedges
- Whole leaf lettuce

MAKE THE DREDGE AND MOP

Combine the dredge ingredients in a shallow bowl so it'll be ready. Prepare the mop, if using, by mixing the Hog Sauce and ketchup together in a small bowl. Once the catfish has been in the cure for 30 minutes, take it out and rinse off the cure. The cure helps set the fish, and it will still be plenty salty even after the rinse—I do not recommend leaving the cure mixture on the fish. Smoke in a wire rack or use whatever fish smoking method you're comfortable with. If you're throwing it on a smoker that's already heated around the 200°F mark, smoke the fish for about 15 to 20 minutes, or until the edges start to change color and look like they've been cooked through. If you're just smoking the catfish, smoke it even lower, in the 150°F to 180°F range for at least 30 minutes. This will let it take on additional smoke character without cooking too much. Remove the catfish from the smoker and transfer to the fridge to cool. You can let it cool to room temperature or fridge temperature, and even refrigerate overnight.

FRY THE CATFISH

When you're ready to fry the smoked fish, set your deep fryer to 325°F or start a cast-iron pan over medium heat. Add enough canola oil to fill your deep fryer or, if using a cast-iron pan, add enough canola oil to come halfway up the side of the dish. (You can also use lard, of course.) While the oil heats up to temperature, dip the catfish in flour, egg wash, and then the Catfish Dredge. Fry the fish for 3 to 5 minutes, or until golden brown.

Serve straight out of the fryer, or lightly brush one side with the Catfish Mop and then serve. Garnish with lemon and a little whole leaf lettuce if you're serving it as a main dish. Or, stack it on a plain white bun with American cheese, bread and butter pickles, and a side of Tartar Sauce (page 122) to recreate our sandwich.

HUSH PUPPIES

🥄 **YIELD:** About 20 small hush puppies

- ¾ cup all-purpose flour
- ¾ cup cornmeal
- 1¼ teaspoons salt
- ¼ teaspoon ground black pepper
- 2½ teaspoons granulated sugar
- ½ teaspoon brown sugar
- ¼ teaspoon onion powder
- ½ teaspoon garlic powder
- 2 teaspoons baking powder
- 4 tablespoons butter, cold and finely diced
- 1 cup buttermilk
- 1 extra-large egg
- ¼ cup finely diced yellow onion
- 1 jalapeño, minced (or smoked jalapeño, optional)

Some may prefer French fries with their fish, but for me it's hard to beat the memory of opening a brown paper bag, stapled shut, and biting into those piping hot hush puppies. At Buxton, it was important for me to be faithful to that memory and serve the best hush puppies. Like perfecting a recipe for soup, the secret to hush puppies is all about dialing in on the right consistency. There's just no way around having to do the final adjustments by sight based on your own experience at your own deep fryer. You'll eventually learn what the mixture should look like, which is a bit on the wet side if you want those hushpuppies perfectly moist. To help foolproof our recipe and make it a bit more forgiving, we stole a technique from making biscuits: add butter to the dry mix. The melted butter breaks down as it cooks and adds moisture and flavor.

PREPARATION

Combine the flour, cornmeal, salt, pepper, sugars, onion and garlic powders, and baking powder in a large mixing bowl. Mix well. Cut in the butter, rubbing into the dry ingredients until they're uniformly mixed (note that some chunks of butter are fine as long as they're evenly dispersed). Whisk together the buttermilk and the eggs in a separate bowl, then make a well in the dry ingredients and add the buttermilk and eggs. Whisk to combine. Fold in the onion and jalapeño. Mix well but avoid overmixing! If you mix the batter too much, you won't get a tender hush puppy.

Heat your deep-fryer or a deep pot filled with canola oil to 350°F. Drop the hush puppy batter into the oil using a small (1-ounce) ice cream scoop or melon baller. Use a slotted spoon to periodically move them around, and take them out when they're golden brown. Set on a wire rack to cool. (You'll want to place some paper towels beneath the wire rack to catch any oil that drips.) Serve with Tartar Sauce (page 122).

recipe continues

TARTAR SAUCE

- ¼ cup sour cream
- ¾ cup mayonnaise
- ⅛ cup finely diced bread and butter pickles
- 1½ teaspoons lemon juice
- ½ teaspoon minced garlic
- ¼ teaspoon Worcestershire sauce
- ¼ teaspoon Texas Pete hot sauce
- ¼ teaspoon salt
- Pinch onion powder
- Pinch garlic powder
- Pinch mustard powder
- Pinch black pepper
- Whole milk to loosen up, if necessary

Combine all ingredients in a medium-size bowl and mix well. Add milk as needed to get the consistency of tartar sauce that you like.

FRIED CHICKEN SANDWICH

YIELD: 5 servings

- 5 chicken breast fillets, about 6 ounces each

Years ago, I worked for a fast-food restaurant known for its chicken, but I've always loved fried chicken. In fact, I have a fried chicken crown tattoo. At Buxton, the chicken sandwich was the sleeper hit of the menu when we opened up. We originally put it on the menu for a couple of reasons— people love fried chicken and we needed a menu item that would ease the strain on limited pit space. But pretty soon it was the fryer that was backing up as order after order for this sandwich came through.

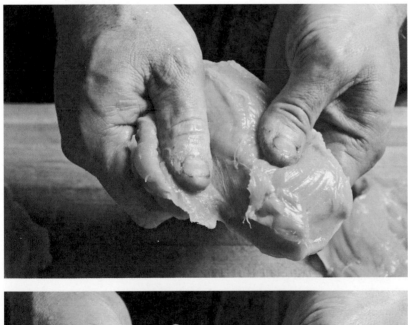

PREPARATION

At Buxton, we start with about 6-ounce portions of chicken where the top lobe of the breast has been removed—otherwise, you'd have a giant chicken sandwich! The first thing to do with your chicken breast, whether you choose to work with a smaller or larger fillet, is to cut it in such a way that it won't curl up in the fryer. To do this, start at the top with a knife and run it down to the pointy end. Then follow that line with your finger as shown. Note that the goal is not to rip the meat; you're just opening the meat up so that when it cooks, it stays flat. If you don't do this, the muscle draws up like a ball when you cook it.

recipe continues

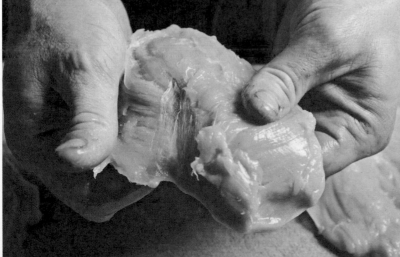

FOR THE CHICKEN BRINE

- 10½ cups warm water
- ½ cup salt
- ½ cup sugar
- ½ tablespoon whole peppercorns
- ½ tablespoon fennel seed
- ½ tablespoon cumin
- ½ tablespoon mustard seed

FOR THE CHICKEN DREDGE

- 2 cups all-purpose flour
- 1 tablespoon plus 1 teaspoon ground black pepper
- 1 tablespoon onion powder
- 1 tablespoon garlic powder
- 1 tablespoon paprika
- 1 tablespoon salt
- 1 tablespoon cornstarch

FOR FRYING

- Canola oil (enough to fill your deep fryer or enough to cover the chicken halfway in a cast-iron pan)
- 1 cup all-purpose flour
- Egg wash (1 cup of buttermilk whisked together with 1 egg)

FOR THE SANDWICHES

- 5 soft white hamburger buns
- 15 bread and butter pickle rounds
- 5 slices American cheese
- About ½ cup Smoked Pimento Cheese (page 127)

MAKE THE BRINE

In a large bowl, combine the warm water, sugar, and salt. Once the sugar and salt are dissolved, add the peppercorns, fennel seed, cumin, and mustard seed and let steep. Add the chicken, cover, and brine in the fridge for at least 8 hours, or overnight.

MAKE THE DREDGE

After the brining is finished, you're ready to fry the chicken. Prepare the dredge by combining the flour, pepper, onion and garlic powders, paprika, salt, and cornstarch in a shallow bowl or pan. Mix well.

FRY THE CHICKEN

Set your deep-fryer to 325°F or get a cast-iron pan and canola oil heating up. (You can also use lard, of course.) While the oil reaches temperature, put the egg wash and flour in their own separate shallow bowls or pans. Remove the chicken from the brine and immediately coat it in flour, egg wash, and then the dredge. Fry it for 4 to 5 minutes or until the internal temperature reaches 165°F. We cook it to that temperature because we serve it immediately. In other words, it never has much of a rest. If your chicken rests at all before serving, you'll want to shoot a little lower with the target fry temperature.

MAKE THE SANDWICH

We serve our sandwich on a white bun toasted in hog fat, though you can choose and toast the buns how you like them best. On the sandwich, we put the pickles on the bottom so the pickle juice seeps a bit into the bread. Then we stack the chicken on top and add the slice of American cheese. The top half of the bun gets a spread of Smoked Pimento Cheese, then you're ready to serve. I also recommend White Barbecue Sauce (page 27) on the side.

SMOKED PIMENTO CHEESE

YIELD: 8 to 10 servings as an appetizer

- ¾ pound extra-sharp Vermont Cheddar (we like Cabot), shredded
- ¼ pound Wisconsin smoked Cheddar, shredded
- ⅛ cup roasted red peppers, finely diced

NOTE: You can also use fermented red peppers.

- ½ cup plus 2 tablespoons mayonnaise (preferably Duke's)
- 3 tablespoons sour cream
- 1 tablespoon spicy whole-grain mustard
- 1 tablespoon Texas Pete hot sauce
- ¼ teaspoon freshly ground black pepper
- ¼ teaspoon herbes de Provence
- ⅛ teaspoon garlic powder
- ⅛ teaspoon onion powder

There are many, many varieties of pimento cheese and I love them all. Wherever I travel, if I see pimento cheese on the menu, I order it. At Buxton, it's the smoked Cheddar that sets our recipe apart. And while we have smokers and we smoke just about everything we can, we actually blend two cheeses available at most grocery stores for our pimento. The Cabot, in particular, has been my favorite everyday cheese for years. Since long before Buxton, I've found that it can make what I think is the best pimento cheese. As far as mayonnaise selection, we use Duke's, but you can substitute with homemade or your favorite brand. At home, I'll sometimes add a splash or two of beer as well.

PREPARATION

Combine all ingredients in a large mixing bowl and stir until well combined. It really is that easy. Smoked Pimento Cheese will store for about 1 week in the fridge.

PIMENTO CHEESE BALL

YIELD: 2 pimento cheese balls, 10 to 12 servings

- 1 pound cream cheese, at room temperature
- ½ pound Smoked Pimento Cheese (page 127)
- 1 teaspoon Worcestershire sauce
- 1 cup smoked pecans (page 66), chopped
- Smoked paprika
- 2 maraschino cherries

For some reason, even though pimento cheese is a Southern thing, cheese logs and cheese balls seem to be more widely recognized. Maybe it's because they have their own regional variations on the recipe. In any case, in my family my aunt and my mom still make cheese balls or logs every year around the holidays and our family recipe uses pimento. This recipe tones down the smoked flavor of our straight Smoked Pimento Cheese (page 127), but the smoke will still come through—especially if you coat it with smoked pecans.

PREPARATION

In the bowl of your stand mixer or in a large mixing bowl (if using a handheld mixer), beat the cream cheese, Smoked Pimento Cheese, and Worcestershire until just combined. Mix in ¼ cup of the chopped pecans until just combined.

Cover the bowl in plastic wrap and chill in the refrigerator for 3 hours. Once the mixture has cooled, divide it into 2 halves. Roll each half into a ball. Roll each ball in the remaining chopped nuts, pressing to make sure the nuts stick. With your thumb, press an indentation in each ball. Sprinkle the top with smoked paprika and place a maraschino cherry in the indentation.

Serve immediately with crackers and raw vegetables or refrigerate, tented in plastic wrap, until ready to serve. Remove from the fridge about an hour before serving.

FERMENTED CHOW-CHOW

YIELD: 2 (1-quart) mason jars full

- 4 cups tightly packed shredded cabbage
- 1 medium carrot, julienned
- 2 green bell peppers, diced
- 1 red bell pepper, diced
- 1 jalapeño, diced
- 1 sweet medium onion, sliced
- 5 cloves garlic, crushed
- ¾ cup sugar
- 1 cup cider vinegar
- 1 teaspoon turmeric
- 1 teaspoon brown mustard seeds
- ⅓ cup kosher salt

Chow-chow is big in the south—I've always considered it an Appalachian take on an Italian giardiniera. Most recipes are built on a cabbage base and include tomatoes, some chili, jalapeño, and bell pepper. The signature yellow color comes from turmeric. The overall flavor is a little sweet and a little sour. At Buxton, our version of chow-chow is lightly fermented as well. The vinegar, sugar, and fermentation flavors all come together for a unique brine. I recommend you try the recipe at various stages as it ferments to find the level of fermentation you like best.

PREPARATION

In a large mixing bowl, combine all the ingredients. Use a wooden spoon or your clean hands to bruise the cabbage. This will help it release water, which will act as the pickling liquid.

Pack the mixture, including all the liquid, into one or more glass mason jars, leaving about an inch of space at the top of each. Cover each jar loosely with its lid. Place the jars out of the way in a room-temperature, dark space for at least 10 days or up to a month. Place them on a sheet pan or plate, as the jars may release some liquid.

Check on the mixture as it ferments, then refrigerate when you like the level of fermentation.

CHRISTMAS QUICHE

YIELD: One 9-inch quiche, 6 to 8 servings

- One 9-inch Cheddar Crust, par-baked as instructed on page 80
- 6 slices bacon
- ¼ cup diced onion
- ½ cup chopped smoked ham
- ½ cup shredded Swiss cheese
- ½ cup shredded sharp Cheddar
- 3 eggs
- 2 egg yolks
- ½ cup milk
- 1 cup heavy cream
- ½ teaspoon dry mustard
- Salt to taste

Hosting brunch can be a hassle, as cooking eggs to order can keep you from enjoying the company of your guests. The answer is breakfast quiche. Bake it just ahead of time and make it part of a breakfast spread with fresh fruit and toast on the side. As this recipe name suggests, this is my favorite quiche to roll out around the holidays as well. The large amount of cheese—including cheese in the crust if you make our recipe on page 180—along with the cream make this quiche quite rich. The extra egg yolks give it a perfect custardy texture. In fact, it's so good there's no need to limit this quiche to brunch. Serve it to a hungry crowd for dinner alongside roasted potatoes or Grits and Gravy (page 114) and a side salad.

PREPARATION

Preheat your oven to 325°F. (Make sure your pie crust is par-baked before making the rest of the quiche.)

In a medium-sized saucepan, cook the bacon until crisp over medium heat, stirring often. Remove the bacon with a spatula or slotted spoon and turn off the burner. Leave the bacon fat in the pan. Crumble the bacon and set aside.

Return the saucepan with the bacon fat to medium heat. Cook the onions and ham in the bacon fat until light brown. Remove the ham and onions from the pan with a slotted spoon or spatula.

Layer the par-baked pie crust starting at the bottom with: Swiss cheese, Cheddar cheese, bacon, ham, and then onions.

In a small mixing bowl, beat the eggs, milk, cream, mustard powder, and salt with a whisk until well combined. Pour the mixture slowly into the layered pie crust.

Bake at 325°F for 40 to 45 minutes or until set. You want the quiche a little jiggly, but not runny. Let it cool for 15 minutes before slicing and serving.

SMOKED DEVILED EGGS

YIELD: 12 deviled egg halves

- 8 to 10 eggs (deviled egg recipe only calls for 6 eggs, but some may break during smoking)
- ¼ cup mayonnaise (preferably Duke's)
- 1 teaspoon Hog Sauce (page 24)
- 1 teaspoon Mustard Sauce (page 29)
- Salt to taste
- Smoked paprika and chopped chives for garnish

The Christmas before Buxton opened, a bunch of friends and future coworkers got together for a holiday party. The night before, I smoked a hog all night. As morning rolled around and a few friends started stopping by, I realized it was breakfast time and we had live coals to use. I carefully placed a dozen eggs around the embers. Where the coals were still too hot, the eggs cracked. But most of the eggs made it through to hard-cooked in about fifteen minutes. We ate those smoky eggs right out of the shell, but it gave me the idea for these Smoked Deviled Eggs.

PREPARATION

Place the eggs in the ashy part of the ember bed. Depending on how hot your pit is, the eggs may cook faster or slower, but they generally take 15 to 20 minutes to cook in a pit that's keeping meat at 200°F to 220°F.

If you get the eggs too close to very hot embers, some may explode. Test a few first or make sure you have extra if you load all of them at once. Test one or two eggs on the early side at 12 to 15 minutes. If they're too runny, sprinkle with salt and enjoy a snack!

Once the eggs are hard-cooked, peel 6 eggs under cool running water. Cut them in half using a sharp knife and scoop out the yolks into a small mixing bowl or food processor. Set the whites aside.

Add the mayonnaise, Hog and Mustard sauces, and salt to the yolks and mix. Use a spoon or a piping bag to fill the halved egg whites with filling. Garnish with chives and paprika. Refrigerate for 2 to 3 hours or until cold enough to serve.

SIDES

Sour Cream Potato Salad with Freezer Peas and Basil

Sal's Macaroni Salad

Collards with "Bacon"

Picnic Potato Salad

Lima Beans in "Gravy"

Cream of Parsnip Soup

Cider Brussels Sprouts with Cracklins

Braised Brussels Sprouts (Vegetarian)

Candied Yams and Parsnips

Oat Crumble

Smoked Cornbread

Red Cabbage Slaw with Blue Cheese

Mom's Marinated Cabbage Slaw

Embered Creamed Corn

Mashed Root Vegetables and Gravy

SOUR CREAM POTATO SALAD WITH FREEZER PEAS AND BASIL

YIELD: 8 servings

- 2 pounds russet potatoes, 1 pound peeled and both pounds diced into ¾-inch pieces
- Cold salted water
- ½ cup sour cream
- ¼ cup mayonnaise (preferably Duke's)
- ¼ cup spicy brown whole grain mustard
- ½ cup chopped scallions
- Juice of ½ lime
- 1 teaspoon garlic powder
- Salt and freshly ground pepper to taste
- ½ cup frozen peas, defrosted
- ½ cup chopped basil

While the potato salad on page 146 is more of a creamy, classic version that goes perfect with our vinegary pulled pork, this salad is tangier. The sour cream, together with a hit of lime juice, gives it the acidity it needs to be a nice, zippy pairing for sweeter barbecue such as sticky ribs or barbecue chicken. The peas and basil are what gives the salad its spring-fresh aroma and flavor, but you can play around with different vegetables and herbs depending on what's in season. For example, I'll switch out the peas or combine them with ramps; I've made this salad with fresh asparagus as well.

PREPARATION

Cook the potatoes by placing them in large pot filled with cold water that's been seasoned with a bit of salt. It's important to start the potatoes in cold water, rather than throwing them into boiling water, as the gradual rise to boiling will ensure evenly cooked potatoes rather than potatoes where the outside layer cooks faster than the dense interior.

Cook the potatoes for 10 to 15 minutes, or until tender. Of course, if you like your potato salad crunchier or a bit softer, cook the potatoes the way you like. Keep in mind that even when running potatoes under cool water that they will continue to cook a little past the point at which you remove them.

While the potatoes are cooking, combine the sour cream, mayonnaise, mustard, scallions, lime juice, and garlic powder in a large mixing bowl. Once the potatoes are cooked and drained, add them to the same bowl while still warm. This way the dressing is soaked up a bit by the hot potatoes. Season to taste with salt and pepper.

Refrigerate for 1 hour, and then stir in the peas and basil. Refrigerate for another hour and serve.

SAL'S MACARONI SALAD

🍴 **YIELD:** 8 servings

- 1¼ pounds dry macaroni
- ¾ cup sour cream
- ¾ cup mayonnaise (preferably Duke's)

NOTE: You can replace ¼ cup of the sour cream and ¼ cup of the mayonnaise with ½ cup Tartar Sauce (see page 122) for additional complexity.

- ½ cup minced smoked green pepper
- ¼ cup minced bread and butter pickles
- ¼ cup minced pickled and smoked red onion
- ¼ red onion, finely diced
- ½ stalk celery, finely diced
- 1 teaspoon onion powder
- 1 teaspoon garlic powder
- 1 teaspoon mustard powder
- 2 teaspoons crushed red pepper
- 1½ teaspoons black pepper
- Salt to taste

Sal is one of our cooks here at Buxton. He's Italian and he came up with our pasta salad recipe—go figure.

However, there's nothing Italian about our macaroni salad. Just like our potato salad, this one is based on the barbecue restaurant classic. At the South Carolina barbecue buffets that I went to while growing up, you always see an assortment of cold salads that includes a house version of creamy pasta salad. We do variations of pasta salad based on what's in season and this is our summertime staple.

PREPARATION

Bring a large pot of water to a boil, season with salt, and cook the pasta until it's al dente. You want the pasta to have a bit of a bite so you don't end up with a mushy pasta salad.

Remove the pasta from the pan and run under cool water. Drain and transfer the pasta into a large mixing bowl.

Add the remaining ingredients and stir well to combine. Taste and adjust the seasoning as needed. Like the potato salad, the pasta salad can be served immediately at close to room temperature or you can refrigerate it until you're ready to serve.

COLLARDS WITH "BACON"

- ½ cup canola oil
- ½ pound Crunchy Hog Bits (see note on page 150) or substitute good-quality bacon such as Nueske's
- 1 sweet onion, sliced
- 10 cloves garlic, sliced
- 1 teaspoon ground black pepper
- 1 teaspoon crushed red pepper
- 1 large bunch collard greens, washed, with stems removed and then roughly chopped
- 3 cups Hog Stock (page 32) or stock of your choosing
- 1 cup cider vinegar
- ½ cup Texas Pete hot sauce
- 1 cup dark brown sugar, tightly packed
- Salt to taste
- Pinch MSG (optional, but recommended if you're using store-bought stock)

Our collards have a lot of flavor, which comes from many ingredients melding together for an hour or more: onion, garlic, chili, cider vinegar, and brown sugar, to name a few. But what really takes our collards over the top is the "bacon." While we started out making our collards with store-bought bacon, we now save the side of the chest as we pick the pig. It's a dry piece that often has a bit of crunch to it. Some people like it mixed into pulled pork, while others don't care for it. But we've found just about everyone loves both the flavor and texture it adds to collards. Whether you use your own "bacon" or a high-quality smoked bacon you buy for this recipe, the long cook time will extract every bit of smoke and pork flavor into the broth. If you're feeling adventurous, you can also switch out the meat completely and make the collards with ham hocks, turkey necks, or other bits of smoked meat you might be looking to use up.

PREPARATION

In a large stockpot, heat the oil and add the hog bits, onion, and garlic. Cook for a few minutes or until the onions have lightly browned. Add the black and red pepper; cook and stir until incorporated. Add the chopped collards, stock, cider vinegar, Texas Pete, sugar, and MSG (again, optional but recommended if you didn't make your own stock). Bring to a boil. Cover with a tight fitting lid and reduce to a simmer. Cook for 1 hour.

How long you need to cook after the first hour depends on how young or tender your collards are. The older collards that you buy as the winter goes on, the ones with larger leaves, will take longer to cook than the early-season collards with smaller leaves. Once the collards are super tender but still have a little bit of bite, or once they're the texture that you like, adjust for seasoning and serve.

PICNIC POTATO SALAD

YIELD: 8 servings

- 2½ pounds russet potatoes, peeled and diced into ¾-inch pieces
- 2 stalks celery, finely diced
- ¾ cups finely diced yellow onion
- 1 or 2 hard-boiled eggs, finely chopped
- ¼ cup minced bread and butter pickles
- 1 cup mayonnaise (preferably Duke's)
- 1½ teaspoons celery seed
- ¼ cup yellow mustard
- 1½ teaspoons freshly ground black pepper
- Salt to taste

Potato salad is a classic side found at just about every barbecue restaurant. We do a variety of seasonal takes on potato salad, but our classic rendition is, well, what many in the South would think of as potato salad: it's mayonnaise and mustard–based with a bit of hard-boiled egg and onion. While we tried to be more inventive—roasting and even smoking potatoes—this ended up the favorite and on the menu pretty much year-round.

PREPARATION

Cook the potatoes by placing them in large pot filled with cold water that's been seasoned with a bit of salt. It's important to start the potatoes in cold water, rather than throwing them into boiling water, as the gradual rise to boiling will ensure evenly cooked potatoes rather than potatoes where the outside layer cooks faster than the dense interior.

Cook the potatoes for 10 to 15 minutes, or until just past an al dente level of bite. Of course, if you like your potato salad crunchier or a bit softer, cook the potatoes the way you like. Keep in mind that even when you run potatoes under cool water, they will continue to cook a little past the point at which you removed them.

Remove the potatoes from the water and run under cool water. Drain and transfer the potatoes into a large mixing bowl.

Add the remaining ingredients and stir well with a large wooden spoon to combine. Taste and adjust the seasoning as needed.

This potato salad can be served right away at close to room temperature or you can refrigerate it until you're ready to serve.

LIMA BEANS IN "GRAVY"

YIELD: 4 to 6 servings

- 1 medium carrot, peeled and finely diced
- 1 stalk celery, finely diced
- 1 medium yellow onion, finely diced
- 3 cloves garlic, crushed
- 1 fresh rosemary sprig, leaves removed and chopped
- 1 (32-ounce) bag frozen lima beans
- Salt, to taste
- 5½ cups filtered water, plus a little extra as needed for consistency
- ½ cup (1 stick) butter
- Juice of 1 lemon

Like frozen peas, frozen lima beans have a surprising amount to offer. If you cook them long enough, they release a natural starch and create a liquid that's very much like gravy. Their consistency also breaks down on the inside while their outer shell remains intact. When you bite into slow-cooked limas, it's almost like you're eating very tiny ravioli. This recipe was designed as a vegetarian side, but you can take it either direction from there. If you eat meat, try adding ham hock or pork for extra flavor. If you're vegan, on the other hand, it won't be quite as rich, but it will taste nearly as good if you omit the butter.

PREPARATION

In a large saucepan, sauté the carrot, celery, onion, garlic, and rosemary over medium heat until they're soft and starting to turn light brown. Add the frozen lima beans, salt, and enough of the 5½ cups of water to cover.

Bring the mixture to a boil, then reduce to a simmer and cook for one hour. Add water as needed to keep the vegetables covered. After an hour, stir in lemon juice and serve.

CREAM OF PARSNIP SOUP

YIELD: 4 to 6 servings

- 2½ pounds parsnips
- ½ large carrot
- 1 medium yellow onion
- ¼ pound (1 stick) unsalted butter
- ½ celery stalk, diced
- 2 to 3 garlic cloves, sliced
- 1 teaspoon fresh thyme leaves
- 2 cups heavy cream
- Salt and pepper to taste
- Crème fraîche, for garnish
- A few pinches fresh thyme leaves, for garnish

This winter recipe is versatile. I really like making it with parsnip, but you can substitute other winter root vegetables if you'd like. Rutabaga, sweet potato, and celery root all make interesting variations on this soup. You can also substitute regular onion in place of the burnt onion, but the burnt onion will give the soup greater depth of flavor. The same thing goes for the garnish: it's extra work to save the peels and fry them as instructed below, but they make for a wonderful finishing touch.

PREPARATION

PREPARE THE VEGETABLES

Peel the parsnips and carrots, reserving the peels. Dice the parsnip and carrot into small cubes.

Rinse and dry the peels, then fry them in canola oil at 300°F until they are crispy. Set these aside, as they'll be used at the end for a garnish.

Burn the onion until it's black on all sides by placing it into a live fire (it's great to do a few of these on days when you're smoking something in the pit). If you're just working in the kitchen, you can carefully burn the onion over a gas burner or by broiling it very near the broiler until black. No matter which way you choose, be very careful and watch the onion the entire time you cook it. You want to heavily char it, not set it on fire.

Once you've charred the onion, let it cool. Cut it in half, with the skin on, and dice half for the soup. The other half is not used in this recipe, so experiment and add some charred onion in place of regular onion in another dish!

MAKE THE SOUP

Melt the butter in a large stockpot. Add the onion, including any burnt skin, along with the celery, carrot, garlic, and thyme. Sauté over medium heat until the vegetables start to turn light brown, about 5 minutes.

Add the parsnips along with the heavy cream and bring the soup to a simmer. Simmer until the parsnips are soft. Using an immersion blender or working in batches with a high-powered conventional blender, blend until very smooth. (The soup should have the consistency of baby food.)

Serve immediately, garnished with the crispy peelings, fresh thyme leaves, and a dollop of crème fraîche.

CIDER BRUSSELS SPROUTS WITH CRACKLINS

YIELD: 4 to 5 servings

FOR THE SAUCE

- ½ to ¾ cups crunchy pork bits or bacon

NOTE: When we pick and pull the hogs, some of the "crunchy bits" on the outside of the hog may get a little too crunchy for pulled pork. We set it aside and save it for recipes like this. If you don't have any crunchy bits on hand, some really nice smoked bacon will be a great substitute.

- 2 tablespoons hog fat or butter
- ½ red onion, diced
- 3 cloves garlic, sliced
- A few pinches fresh thyme
- 1½ Granny Smith apples, diced
- Salt and pepper
- ¼ cup cider vinegar
- 1 cup apple cider
- ½ cup Hog Stock (page 32)

We roast our brussels sprouts in a pan that we set up on top of the coals, right under the pig. This is the ultimate position for roasting: not only do they pick up char and smoke flavor from the coals, but they get additional seasoning from the fat dripping down off the pig right above them. Of course, that means you should consider these brussels sprouts if you're doing a whole hog. On the other hand, these brussels sprouts are plenty good even without such a preferential cooking treatment. For a vegetarian take on brussels sprouts, see page 153.

PREPARATION

MAKE THE SAUCE

In a skillet, render the crunchy pork bits in a pan of hog fat or fry the bacon for about two minutes over high heat. Add the onion, garlic, and thyme and cook until soft. Add the apples, season with salt and pepper, and cook for 2 more minutes. Deglaze the pan with the cider vinegar; add the apple cider and the stock. Adjust the heat so that the mixture is at a low boil. When the volume reduces by about a third, the sauce is ready. Turn off the heat. Measure out ½ cup to use, and refrigerate any remaining sauce to use later.

recipe continues

FOR THE BRUSSELS SPROUTS

- 1 pound brussels sprouts
- ½ cup brussels sprouts sauce
- Handful of cracklins, for garnish

NOTE: We render all of the fat and skin scraps we collect when we pick the hogs. Rendering—a.k.a. frying—these bits produces "cracklins." You can also find cracklins in most convenience or grocery stores.

- Salt and pepper, to taste

MAKE THE BRUSSELS SPROUTS

Roast the brussels sprouts in the oven at 400°F, stirring often, until the sprouts are deeply browned, about 20 minutes. Transfer them to a large mixing bowl. Toss with the reserved ½ cup of sauce. Season with salt and pepper to taste.

Serve immediately, garnished with the cracklins.

BRAISED BRUSSELS SPROUTS (VEGETARIAN)

YIELD: 4 to 5 servings

- 1 tablespoon canola oil
- 1 tablespoon unsalted butter
- ½ small onion, sliced
- ¾ pound brussels sprouts
- 4 garlic cloves, sliced
- 1½ teaspoon kosher salt
- ¼ teaspoon black pepper
- ½ cup cider vinegar
- ¼ cup Texas Pete hot sauce
- ¼ cup sugar
- 1 cup water

While it's hard to beat brussels sprouts slow-cooked with meat, the truth is that brussels sprouts are hearty little balls packed with flavor. They can shine just fine without meat. I designed this dish for the vegetarians. The mixture of vinegar, hot sauce, sugar, onion, and spices blends together and becomes a sort of broth or pot likker. Try serving these at your next get-together and I guarantee you'll please vegetarians and meat eaters alike.

PREPARATION

Heat the oil and butter over medium-high heat in a medium-size sauté pan. Add the onion and cook until it's golden brown. Add the brussels sprouts and cook until they start to brown. Then add the garlic, salt, and pepper and cook for about 2 minutes. Add the vinegar, Texas Pete, sugar, and a cup of water. Bring the mixture to a boil, reduce to a simmer, and cook uncovered for about 30 minutes or until about a cup of liquid remains and the brussels sprouts are tender.

CANDIED YAMS AND PARSNIPS

🍴 **YIELD:** 8 to 10 servings

FOR THE SAUCE

- 1 cup (2 sticks) butter
- 1¼ cups brown sugar
- ½ cup granulated sugar
- 1 tablespoon vanilla
- Zest of ½ orange
- ½ vanilla pod, scraped
- ¼ cup sorghum
- ⅓ cup water
- Pinch salt
- Pinch cinnamon
- Pinch nutmeg
- Juice of ½ lemon

FOR THE CASSEROLE

- 2 medium-size sweet potatoes, peeled and diced
- 5 parsnips, peeled and diced
- Pinch salt
- 1 tablespoon butter
- 1 cup water

Our candied yams are roasted in a special sauce, which creates a casserole that's delicious right out of the oven. But we don't stop there. When it's time to serve one of our tables, we take a scoop of that casserole and sauté it with a bit of additional sauce. To finish it off, we melt a house-made marshmallow (page 176) with a blowtorch over top and add some crumbled oats and pecans, almost like a streusel. At home, you can use the topping on page 155 or toasted pecans. Don't skip the toasted marshmallow—even if you have to go store-bought.

PREPARATION
MAKE THE SAUCE

Melt the butter and sugars in a medium-size saucepan over medium heat. Add the rest of the ingredients, bring to a simmer, and cook for 5 minutes, stirring constantly. Turn off the heat and let cool. Reserve 1 cup of the sauce for the sautéing step. The mixture will keep in the fridge for 2 weeks.

MAKE THE CASSEROLE

Cover the sweet potato and parsnip with the remaining sauce, salt, and butter in a large roasting pan. Add water and cover. Bake at 375°F for 30 minutes or until the sweet potatoes and parsnips are soft.

SAUTÉ AND SERVE THE CASSEROLE

Over medium heat, working in batches if necessary, sauté the casserole with enough of the remaining sauce to coat the vegetables for 2 minutes or until the mixture is hot enough to serve.

Divide the casserole into 8 to 10 soup cups or small bowls. Top with Oat Crumble (see page 155), pecans, and a marshmallow (page 176). Toast the marshmallow with a torch or lighter and serve.

OAT CRUMBLE

- 1 cup plus 2 tablespoons all-purpose flour
- ½ cup old-fashioned rolled oats
- 6 tablespoons light brown sugar, firmly packed
- 2 tablespoons plus 2 teaspoons granulated sugar
- ¼ teaspoon cinnamon
- ¼ teaspoon kosher salt
- ½ cup (1 stick) butter, room temperature

In a medium bowl, combine all the ingredients. Mix by hand until small clumps begin to form and the butter is evenly mixed with the dry ingredients. At this point, you can refrigerate or freeze the mixture if you're not using it immediately. When you're ready to bake it, sprinkle the cold topping onto a greased baking sheet. Bake at 350°F until golden brown and crispy, approximately 20 minutes.

SMOKED CORNBREAD

YIELD: 10-inch skillet of cornbread

- 1¼ cups cornmeal, smoked (see page 61)
- ½ cup (1 stick) butter at room temperature
- 1 egg
- 1¼ cups all-purpose flour
- 2 cups buttermilk

Just like with our grits (page 114), for our cornbread we use Farm and Sparrow cornmeal. It provides a nice coarse texture and great corn flavor. As with grits, seek out the best-quality cornmeal you can find. It will make a difference in your cornbread.

Before we bake with the cornmeal, we smoke it (see page 61), which adds another layer of flavor to our cornbread. You'll find that this cornbread not only eats great on its own—it has a complex nutty flavor—it works very well in other recipes. For example, we use it around Thanksgiving to make cornbread dressing.

PREPARATION

As mentioned above, it's important to smoke the cornmeal according to the instructions on page 61 before making this cornbread.

When your cornmeal is ready, preheat your oven to 350°F. Grease a 10-inch cast iron pan with hot fat or butter.

In the bowl of your stand mixer (recommended) or in a large mixing bowl (if using a hand mixer), cream the butter using the whisk attachment at medium speed.

Add the egg and continue to whip until incorporated. Add the cornmeal and flour; beat on a low speed until the mixture resembles mashed potatoes. Slowly add the buttermilk while continuing to beat on low.

Transfer to the greased cast-iron pan. Bake at 350°F for 20 to 25 minutes or until golden brown. The interior of the cornbread should be dry or mostly dry if you insert a cake tester, but the cornbread will continue to cook a bit once you remove it from the oven, thanks to the cast-iron skillet.

Let cool at least 10 minutes, then cut and serve.

RED CABBAGE SLAW WITH BLUE CHEESE

YIELD: 8 to 10 servings

- 1 medium head red cabbage, finely sliced
- 2 medium carrots, peeled and shredded
- 1 small sweet onion, finely sliced
- 1½ teaspoons salt
- 1½ cups mayonnaise (preferably Duke's)
- ½ cup sour cream
- ¼ cup spicy brown whole grain mustard
- 2 tablespoons cider vinegar
- ½ teaspoon celery seed
- ¼ cup sugar
- ½ teaspoon freshly ground black pepper
- Juice of 1 lemon
- 1½ cups crumbled smoked or regular blue cheese (go for a high-quality cheese in this recipe)
- 1 cup chopped herbs, such as parsley, chives, and scallions

While the tangy coleslaw on page 160 is based on a family recipe, this red cabbage slaw is one I created on my own. I wanted to come up with a creamy slaw, but as I'm not a fan of traditional slaws, I turned to one of my favorite creamy cheeses. Because blue cheese brings a lot of flavor with it in addition to its creaminess, this coleslaw can really pack a punch. In addition to going great with hearty and sweet barbecue like Pit Beef (page 92), it can be piled on smoked chicken or pork for some very tasty tacos.

PREPARATION

Combine the cabbage, carrot, and onion in a large mixing bowl. Add the salt and let sit for 2 hours. Drain off any liquid that has come out.

In a separate bowl, mix the mayonnaise, sour cream, mustard, vinegar, celery seed, sugar, and lemon juice. Add this dressing to the vegetables and mix well. Stir in the crumbled blue cheese and herbs. Refrigerate for 2 hours, then serve.

MOM'S MARINATED CABBAGE SLAW

YIELD: 8 to 10 servings

- 1 large head green cabbage, thinly sliced
- 1 large sweet onion, thinly sliced
- 1 large green bell pepper, diced
- ¾ cup sugar
- 1 teaspoon salt
- ¾ cup cider vinegar
- ¾ cup canola oil
- 2 tablespoons sugar
- 1 teaspoon mustard powder
- 1 teaspoon garlic powder
- 1 teaspoon ground black pepper

Barbecue and coleslaw are like French fries and ketchup—most people see the two as going hand in hand, but there are a few people who disagree. When it comes to classic coleslaw, I am one of those in the minority. But I've found there are plenty of alternative slaws out there that I enjoy and that have a home on our menu.

This slaw is based on a recipe that my mom makes—it's almost a marinated salad of sorts. The hot liquid cooks the vegetables just a bit and then the overnight marinade lets the flavors come together. After that, it can last another day or two in the fridge as it continues to change texture and flavor a bit. It's almost like fresh pickles in that way. As this is a tangy slaw, it's a nice one to serve with sweeter barbecue, like ribs.

PREPARATION

In a large bowl, layer the cabbage, onion, and bell pepper. Cover with ¾ cup sugar and the salt.

In a medium saucepan, combine the cider vinegar, canola oil, sugar, mustard powder, garlic powder, and black pepper. Over high heat, bring to a boil, then pour over the cabbage mixture. My mom explicitly told me not to stir at this point; it's important to refrigerate it overnight first.

The next day, take the coleslaw out of the fridge, stir, and serve.

EMBERED CREAMED CORN

YIELD: 4 to 6 servings

- 10 ears corn
- 2 poblano peppers
- 1 jalapeño pepper
- ¼ pound (1 stick) butter
- 1 Vidalia onion, finely diced
- 3 cloves garlic, crushed
- 1 teaspoon ground cumin
- Salt and pepper to taste
- 1 cup heavy cream
- ¼ cup water
- ½ cup sour cream
- Juice of 1 lime
- ¼ cup chopped basil
- ¼ cup chopped cilantro

Creamed corn might be something you think of as coming from a can, but this recipe will open your eyes to a completely different style of the dish. When corn is in season, you can't beat the flavor. I often throw a few ears of corn on the pit while I'm cooking meat throughout the summer. This recipe is written with that in mind (you'll want to ember the vegetables as on page 105). If you want to try cooking the vegetables another way, the flavor will be different but still much more delicious than any canned version.

PREPARATION

EMBER THE VEGETABLES

Shuck the corn. Ember the corn and poblano and jalapeño peppers by placing them directly over coals. Flip them regularly until all sides are charred. You may need to blow or fan the coals to help them stay hot and glowing. This can also help remove ash from the vegetables as you cook. (For more on ember roasting vegetables, see page 105.)

Cut the kernels from the cob and transfer to a mixing bowl. Use the back of a knife to squeeze all of the corn "milk" from the cobs into the mixing bowl as well. Remove the seeds from the peppers and dice, keeping them separate from the corn.

recipe continues

MAKE THE CREAMED CORN

Melt the butter in a medium saucepan over medium heat. Add the peppers, onion, and garlic. Season with the cumin; add salt and pepper to taste. Slowly cook the vegetables over medium heat until they're light brown. Add the corn, cream, and water; bring the mixture to a simmer. Simmer for 5 minutes and then turn off the heat. Stir in the sour cream, lime juice, and half of the basil and cilantro.

Serve immediately, garnished with the other half of the herbs.

MASHED ROOT VEGETABLES AND GRAVY

YIELD: 6 to 8 servings

- 2 russet potatoes, peeled and diced into ¾-inch pieces
- 1 large sweet potato, peeled and diced into ¾-inch pieces
- 1 turnip, peeled and diced into ¾-inch pieces
- 1 carrot, peeled and diced into ¾-inch pieces
- 1 parsnip, peeled and diced into ¾-inch pieces
- ½ cup (1 stick) butter
- 2 cups milk
- 1 cup heavy cream
- ½ cup sour cream
- Salt and pepper to taste
- Hog Gravy (page 114) or your favorite gravy, for garnish
- Fresh herbs such as parsley and chive, for garnish

Just about everyone has made mashed potatoes. Yet for some reason, not many people I know have mashed other root vegetables. I'm not sure where I first picked up the idea myself, but I've been making these in commercial kitchens since my very first job as a chef. As with the Cream of Parsnip Soup (page 149), feel free to substitute vegetables for variations on this recipe. You can really make this with any root vegetables if you shoot for a ratio of something like one-third russets, one-third sweet roots, and one-third mixed, flavorful roots.

PREPARATION

Put all of the vegetables in a medium-size saucepan. Add the butter, milk, and cream; bring to a boil. As soon as it reaches a boil, reduce to a simmer and cook for 25 minutes or until the potatoes are fork tender. At this point, remove the pan from the heat. Strain immediately, reserving the liquid.

With a food mill or potato masher, mash the root vegetables until they reach your desired smoothness. Add the reserved cooking liquid slowly and stir. Stop adding liquid when the mash reaches the consistency of thick mashed potatoes. Add the sour cream; salt and pepper to taste.

Serve garnished with Hog Gravy (page 114) and fresh herbs.

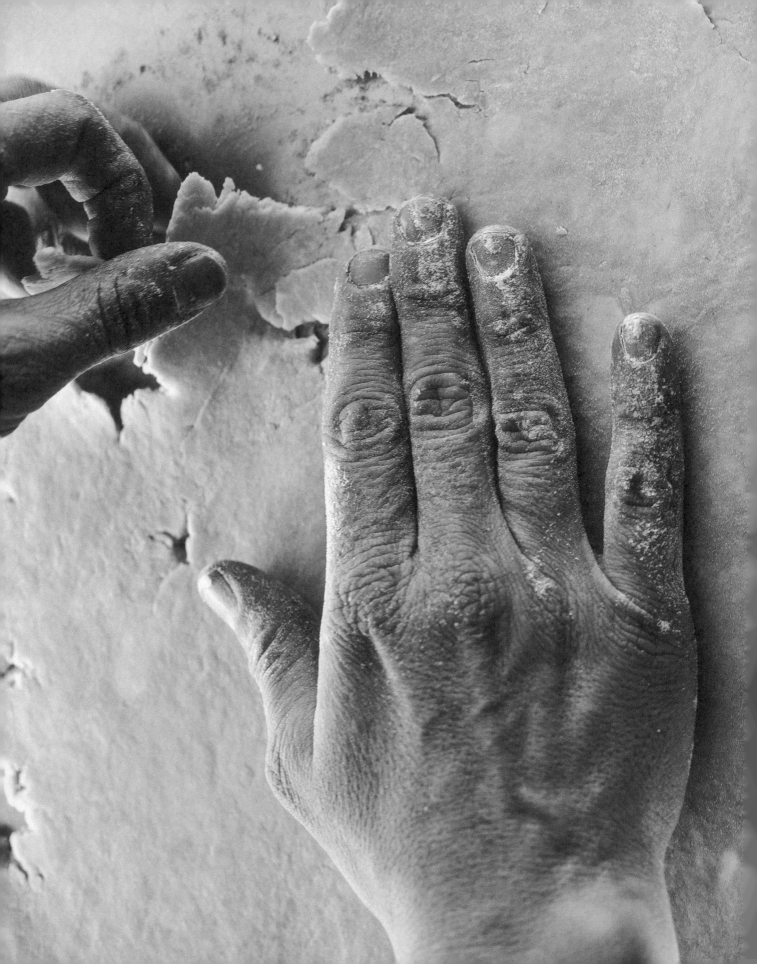

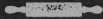

DESSERTS

Bunilla Wafers

Buxton Kids' Gelatin

S'mores

Graham Crackers

Marshmallows

Pie Crusts

Super Flaky Pie Crust

Rye Crust

Cheddar Crust

Brown Butter Crust

Brown Butter

Banana Pudding Pie

Bunilla Wafer Crust

Brown Sugar Meringue

Grape Hull Pie

Rye Crumble

Buttermilk Pie

Pecan Pie

Apple Cheddar Pie

Chocolate Chess Pie

Chocolate Short Crust

Cherry Yum Yum Pie

Buxton's Pound Cake

BUNILLA WAFERS

YIELD: Approximately 100 cookies, which gives you 60 cookies for 2 (9-inch) Bunilla Wafer Crusts (page 186), with an extra 40 cookies left over

- Butter or shortening for greasing pans
- 2 cups (4 sticks) unsalted butter, at room temperature
- 2 cups sugar
- 1½ teaspoons salt
- 6 egg whites
- 2 whole eggs
- 1 tablespoon vanilla extract
- ½ vanilla bean, seeds scraped from the pod
- 5⅔ cups all-purpose flour

Our Bunilla Wafers taste just like the classic vanilla wafers you'd buy at the store. Some might question whether that's a good thing—why make something you can buy? But we believe in making everything we can from scratch, and there are no preservatives in these cookies. Of course, making them yourself also means you can change the size or shape, or bake them a bit less or more, to your liking.

PREPARATION

Preheat your oven to 325°F and grease 4 sheet trays (or 2 trays if working in batches). Combine the butter, sugar, and salt in the mixing bowl of your stand mixer (recommended) or other mixing bowl. Mix over low speed, using the paddle attachment to cream. (Don't mix at a high speed or you'll incorporate a lot of air.)

In a separate bowl, whisk the egg whites, eggs, vanilla extract, and vanilla bean seeds by hand, then incorporate slowly into the butter mixture. Keep the mixer at a low speed as you add the egg and vanilla mixture.

Still at a low speed, add the flour all at once. Blend until uniformly combined. Don't overmix, but make sure there are no streaks in the batter. Scrape the bowl down to ensure the batter is evenly mixed.

Use a piping bag with a round tip to pipe the cookies or use a small cookie scoop (about ½ ounce) or tablespoon to scoop the cookies onto the greased sheet tray. If you're using a piping bag, note that it's easy to pipe the cookies when the batter is freshly mixed. If you refrigerate the batter, I'd recommend bringing it back to room temperature before piping.

Bake at 325°F for 10 to 12 minutes, rotating halfway through, or until the edges are golden brown but the center is still a bit lighter in color.

NOTE: If you don't want to bake all the dough at once, you can freeze the dough for up to 1 month.

BUXTON KIDS' GELATIN

YIELD: 4½ cups, or enough to fill about 12 (3-ounce) molds

FOR HOG TROTTER GELATIN

- 2 hog trotters, raw and unsmoked
- 1 cup 100 percent fruit juice
- ½ cup sugar
- 1 tablespoon lemon juice

NOTE: We use fresh muscadine grape juice when in season. Store-bought grape, apple, cherry, or lime juice can also work well as long as you buy high-quality juice that is not sweetened with additional sugar. Also, make sure you chill your juice if you use it to bloom gelatin packets.

FOR GRANULATED GELATIN OR SHEETS

- 3 cups 100 percent juice, ice-cold (see Note above)
- 1 cup water, ice cold
- 2 tablespoons granulated gelatin or 6 sheets gelatin
- ½ cup sugar
- 1 tablespoon lemon juice

I've always been a big Jell-O fan and have been collecting vintage molds for years. My friend Nate Allen, the owner and chef at Knife and Fork in Spruce Pine, North Carolina, was the one who gave us the idea for making our own version of Jell-O. On an early visit to Buxton, he noticed that we had enough hog trotters leftover to make gelatin. He left us a note explaining how to do it, which included the wonderful phrase "cook them 'til they explode" . . . so that's what we did.

Once we had gelatin, it was a short jump to making our own sweet treat. The hog trotter gelatin has a subtle savory flavor, which we've found works well with apple and grape flavors in particular. Also, if you're using the trotter gelatin, note that the gel will be a bit cloudy. You might think that kids would be less excited about a cloudy, pale gel than the processed kind made with bright food coloring, but we've found that the sweet wiggling dessert brings a smile to ten out of ten kids as it jiggles its way to the table.

PREPARATION USING HOG TROTTER GELATIN

To make the hog trotter gelatin, place two raw unsmoked hog trotters in a large pot and cover with water. Bring to a boil, then reduce heat to a medium, less-aggressive boil. Cook until the trotters begin to fall apart. This could take between 2 and 4 hours. Keep replenishing water as needed to keep them covered.

Once the trotters have fallen apart, allow the remaining water to slowly boil away, leaving behind only liquid trotter gelatin and bits of bone and skin. Remove the pot from the heat and cool at room temperature for an hour before pouring the mixture through a strainer. Chill the strained mixture overnight. The next day, you'll see the fat on top and the gelatin underneath. Remove the fat, reserving the trotter gelatin. You can warm the mixture back up and strain it through cheesecloth if you want to clarify it.

Measure 3 cups of gelatin and combine with 1 cup of fruit juice. In a medium-size pot, heat the sugar with the gelatin mixture until the sugar is dissolved. Add the lemon juice and stir until well combined; turn off the heat. The goal is to just warm and melt the gelatin. You don't have to use a

thermometer, but gelatin melts at 86°F and begins to set up at 68°F.

Strain the liquid into a mixing bowl with a spout, a pitcher, or a very large measuring cup, then transfer to your molds. Chill the gelatin in molds overnight or until set (generally at least 4 hours).

PREPARATION USING GRANULATED GELATIN OR SHEETS

To bloom the granulated gelatin, pour the 3 cups of ice-cold juice and 1 cup of ice-cold water into a mixing bowl. Sprinkle all the gelatin on top. Allow the gelatin to evenly absorb the liquid for 5 minutes or according to your package directions.

If you're using sheet gelatin, plunge each sheet into a bowl of ice water.

Allow the sheets to remain in the ice water for 5 minutes, or until the sheets rehydrate (bloom) and are soft, rubbery, and pliable in texture. Remove bloomed sheets from the ice water, squeeze gently to remove any excess water, and transfer to your mixing bowl with the 3 cups of ice-cold juice and 1 cup ice-cold water.

In a medium-size pot, heat the sugar with the gelatin mixture until the sugar is dissolved. Add the lemon juice and stir until well combined; turn off the heat. The goal is to just warm and melt the gelatin. You don't have to use a thermometer, but gelatin melts at 86°F and begins to set up at 68°F.

Strain the liquid into a mixing bowl with a spout, a pitcher, or a very large measuring cup, then transfer to your molds. Chill in molds overnight or until set (generally at least 4 hours).

S'MORES

The wow-factor of having a burning stick of marshmallows coming through the dining room is what started us on the path to making our own. From there, it was just a hop, skip, and a jump to making our own s'mores—and we mean that literally. We only have to walk about a block to source the perfect fresh chocolate from French Broad Chocolate Lounge. And Ashley Capps, our pastry chef, almost always has fresh graham crackers downstairs. Since we have a fire burning all the time, roasting them to order is convenient any time of day. Even if you're planning to make your s'mores the next time you camp, there's no need to go store-bought for the marshmallows and graham crackers. Both the recipes that follow store well, so they can be made a few days ahead of time.

GRAHAM CRACKERS

YIELD: 20 graham crackers (a 12×17-inch baking sheet full)

- ⅓ cup plus 2 tablespoons cake flour
- ⅓ cup bread flour
- ½ cup plus 1 tablespoon whole wheat flour
- ¼ cup brown sugar, tightly packed
- ¼ teaspoon cinnamon
- ¼ teaspoon salt
- ¼ teaspoon baking soda
- ⅓ teaspoon baking powder
- ¼ cup (½ stick) unsalted butter, at room temperature
- 2 tablespoons molasses
- 1 tablespoon plus 1½ teaspoons milk
- ¼ teaspoon vanilla extract
- Turbinado and granulated sugar for sprinkling atop crackers

PREPARATION

Preheat the oven to 325°F. Combine the flours, brown sugar, cinnamon, salt, baking soda, and baking powder in a food processor. Pulse them to combine. Add the butter and pulse until the mixture is uniform but still mealy. You should see small pieces of butter in the mixture.

In a small bowl, whisk together the molasses, milk, and vanilla. Add them to the food processor and pulse until well combined.

Remove the mixture from the food processor and shape it into a rectangle. Wrap with plastic wrap and chill for about 30 minutes. Remove from the fridge and place the dough between 2 large sheets of parchment paper. Roll out with a rolling pin to a width of 10×16 inches (this will fit just inside the baking sheet). Remove the parchment. If the parchment is sticking, place back into the fridge for a few minutes and try again. Use a pastry wheel to cut the dough into 20 pieces (2×4 inches each). Use a fork to dock each graham cracker decoratively. Sprinkle with a mix of turbinado and granulated sugars. Bake at 325°F for 12 to 15 minutes or until lightly browned and set.

MARSHMALLOWS

YIELD: 8-inch square baking dish full of marshmallows

- Oil or butter for pan
- Powdered sugar for coating the baking dish and for topping
- 1½ cups ice-cold water
- 8 gelatin sheets or 2 tablespoons plus 2 teaspoons granulated gelatin
- 1 tablespoon vanilla extract
- 1 vanilla bean, seeds scraped from the pod
- 2¼ cups granulated sugar
- 1½ cups corn syrup
- ½ teaspoon salt
- ¾ cup water

PREPARATION

Prepare an 8-inch square baking dish by lightly oiling it and dusting it generously with powdered sugar. Set aside. Prepare your stand mixer (recommended) or hand mixer by making sure you have a clean mixing bowl ready and a whisk attachment inserted.

To bloom the granulated gelatin, pour the 1½ cups of ice cold water into the mixing bowl. Sprinkle all of the gelatin granules on top of the water. Allow the gelatin to evenly absorb the water for 5 minutes or according to your package directions. If you're using sheet gelatin, plunge each sheet into a bowl of ice water. Allow the sheets to remain in the ice water for five minutes, or until the sheets rehydrate (bloom) and are soft, rubbery, and pliable in texture. Remove bloomed sheets from the ice water, squeeze gently to remove any excess water, and transfer to your mixing bowl with 1½ cups of ice-cold water.

Once the granulated gelatin has absorbed all of the water or once the sheet gelatin is ready in the mixing bowl, add the vanilla extract and vanilla bean seeds.

In a medium-size pot, combine the sugar, corn syrup, salt, and ¾ cup water. Bring the mixture to a boil and continue to heat to 240°F. Pour this syrup directly into the mixing bowl containing the gelatin and vanilla mixture. Whip on medium speed for 2 minutes, then increase the speed to high and whip until thick, about 4 minutes. The mixture will still be very warm and pourable.

Pour the marshmallow mixture into the prepared baking dish. Dust lightly with additional powdered sugar. Place in a cool location to dry overnight. The next day, cut the marshmallows into 1-inch squares using a pizza cutter, pastry wheel, or paring knife. I recommend coating your cutting tool in powdered sugar to make the cutting process easier. Toss the marshmallows with additional powdered sugar, as needed, to keep them from sticking together once cut.

You can serve the marshmallows immediately at this point or you can store cut marshmallows in an airtight container for about 3 weeks.

PIE CRUSTS

SUPER FLAKY PIE CRUST

YIELD: 2 crusts for 2 9-inch pies

- 2 cups plus ¾ cup all-purpose flour
- 1½ teaspoons salt
- 1 teaspoon sugar
- ½ cup (1 stick) unsalted butter, cold and diced
- ⅓ cup hog fat or lard, or an additional ⅓ cup butter
- ⅓ cup ice-cold water combined with 1 teaspoon vinegar

Our pastry chef, Ashley, worked for two seasons at Farm and Sparrow, a local bakery. She spent many days laminating puff pastry and croissant dough by hand. Hour after hour, she folded Amish butter into dough. She says it's that experience that made her such a fanatic for beautiful, flaky pie crust. Ashley says, "Texture is a huge part of an enjoyable pie, and there's nothing that can ruin that faster than a soggy bottom crust." I have to say I agree.

PREPARATION

Sift the flour into the mixing bowl of a stand mixer (recommended) or into a large mixing bowl if using a handheld mixer. Add the salt and sugar to the flour, then add the cold butter pieces. Using the paddle attachment, mix on low speed until butter is medium dice–size. Add the hog fat a little at a time over the course of 1 to 2 minutes. Add the water-vinegar mixture and mix on low for 1 to 2 minutes until the dough begins to come together. The dough should be shaggy and a bit dry in appearance, but you should be able to form it into a mass by hand. The butter and fat streaks should still be visible.

Divide the dough into 2 portions. Shape into square, flat pieces. Wrap and refrigerate 30 minutes to rest. Roll the squares thin and laminate the dough 2 times to achieve a superior flaky crust. Chill the dough after laminating to relax it, then move on to lining the pans.

NOTE: Laminating is essentially folding the dough over on itself to create layers. Use a rolling pin to roll out the dough twice the size it needs to be, fold it over on itself, and repeat once more for this pie crust. While for some pastries you would add additional butter as you laminate, this lamination does not call for extra butter—it will work with the large flecks of butter and fat in the pie dough.

If you're making the Buttermilk Pie (page 191), now is the time to par-bake or blind-bake the crust. Remove the dough after it's had enough time to chill and roll it out into 2 circles (12 inches). Line the pie shells, trim the edges, crimp the edges, and freeze.

Line the interior of the frozen pie shell with parchment paper and fill with pie weights or dried beans. Bake at 350°F for 20 minutes, remove from the oven, and let cool for 5 minutes. Remove the parchment and beans. Return to the oven to dry out the bottom of the pie shell, approximately 5 to 7 minutes.

RYE CRUST

🥄 **YIELD:** 2 crusts for 2 9-inch pies

- 1⅔ cup bread flour
- 1 cup plus 2 tablespoons rye flour
- 1¼ teaspoon salt
- 1 teaspoon sugar
- 1 cup (2 sticks) unsalted butter, cold and diced
- ⅓ cup ice-cold water combined with 1 tablespoon vinegar

This crust, for us, was all about making a pie as local as possible. Our pastry chef, Ashley, found a recipe from the 1800s for muscadine grape pie with rye crust and clabbered cream. As she developed our own Grape Hull Pie (page 188), she decided to go with a rye crust as well because she could source locally grown and ground rye flour. The slight sourness of the rye plays very well with the grapes. Try this crust with other sweet pies as well—you'll find it brings a bit of balance.

PREPARATION

Sift the flours into the mixing bowl of a stand mixer (recommended) or into a large mixing bowl if using a handheld mixer or mixing by hand. Add the salt and sugar to the flour, then add the cold butter pieces. Using the paddle attachment, mix on low speed until butter is pea-size.

Add the water-vinegar mixture and mix on low for 1 to 2 minutes until the dough begins to come together. The dough should be shaggy and a bit dry in appearance, but you should be able form it into a mass by hand. The butter streaks should still be visible.

Divide the dough into 2 portions. Shape into square, flat pieces. Wrap and refrigerate 30 minutes to rest. Roll the squares thin and laminate the dough 2 times to achieve a superior flaky crust. Chill the dough after laminating to relax it, then move on to lining the pans.

NOTE: Laminating is essentially folding the dough over on itself to create layers. Use a rolling pin to roll out the dough twice the size it needs to be, fold it over on itself, and repeat once more for this pie crust. While for some pastries you would add additional butter as you laminate, this lamination does not call for extra butter—it will work with the large flecks of butter in the pie dough.

If you're making the Grape Hull Pie (page 188), now is the time to par-bake or blind-bake the crust. Remove the dough after it's had enough time to chill, then roll out into 2 circles (12 inches). Line the pie shells, trim the edges, crimp the edges, and freeze.

Line the interior of the frozen pie shell with parchment paper and fill with pie weights or dried beans. Bake at 350°F for 20 minutes, remove from the oven, and let cool for 5 minutes. Remove the parchment and beans and preheat the oven to 325°F. Return to the oven to dry out the bottom of the pie shell, approximately 5 to 7 minutes.

Opposite: Super Flaky Pie Crust

CHEDDAR CRUST

🥄 **YIELD:** 2 crusts (top and bottom) for one 9-inch pie

- 2½ cups plus ⅓ cup all-purpose flour
- 1 teaspoon salt
- 1½ teaspoons sugar
- 1 cup (2 sticks) unsalted butter, cold and diced
- ¼ cup white or yellow sharp Cheddar, grated
- 6 tablespoons ice-cold water combined with ½ tablespoon vinegar

This is the crust that makes our Apple Cheddar Pie (page 195) so unique. It has a nice Cheddar flavor, but it's not so strong that it will overwhelm a sweet fruit filling. This crust is also a natural fit for savory pies or a quiche, such as the Christmas Quiche on page 132.

PREPARATION

Sift the flour into the mixing bowl of a stand mixer (recommended) or into a large mixing bowl if you're using a handheld mixer. Add the salt and sugar to the flour, then add the cold butter pieces. Using the paddle attachment, mix on low speed until the butter begins to reduce in size to walnut-size pieces. Add the grated Cheddar and mix until just combined.

Add the water-vinegar mixture and mix on low for 1 to 2 minutes until the dough begins to come together. The dough should be shaggy and a bit dry in appearance, but you should be able to form it into a mass by hand. Butter streaks should still be visible.

Divide the dough into 2 equal portions. Shape each portion into a round, flat disk. Wrap and refrigerate 30 minutes to rest.

If you're making the Apple Cheddar Pie (page 195), roll each portion out to approximately an 11-inch circle. Line a pie pan with 1 dough circle, making sure to press the edges into the pie pan so that the dough is flush with the pan—no pockets. At this point, the lined pie pan and the extra rolled circle (which will be the top) can be refrigerated until you're ready to assemble the pie.

If you're making the Christmas Quiche (page 132), roll 1 dough portion out to approximately an 11-inch circle. (You will have 1 portion of dough left over, which you can wrap well and freeze for later use.) To par-bake or blind-bake the crust, line a pie pan with the dough circle, making sure to press the edges into the pie pans so that the dough is flush with the pan—no pockets—and freeze.

Once the dough is frozen, line the interior of each pie shell with parchment paper and fill with pie weights or dried beans. Bake at 375°F for 20 minutes, remove from the oven, and let cool for 5 minutes. Remove the parchment and beans and set the oven to 325°F. Return to the oven to dry out the bottom of the pie shell, approximately 5 to 7 minutes.

Opposite: Super Flaky Pie Crust

BROWN BUTTER CRUST

YIELD: 2 crusts for 2 9-inch pies

- 3 cups all-purpose flour
- 1 tablespoon whole wheat flour
- 2 teaspoons salt
- 1 teaspoon sugar
- ⅓ cup brown butter (see 183), cold and diced
- ⅔ cup unsalted butter, cold and diced
- ½ cup ice water combined with 1 teaspoon vodka

NOTE: Remove ice before measuring the ½ cup water.

If you've ever smelled brown butter, you already know why we developed a crust recipe that features the flavor. Compared to crusts with regular butter, brown butter adds a lot of depth. The challenge is that brown butter has a different melting point and different properties from regular butter, but we figured out the proper ratios through trial and error. Note that as you're mixing the dough, the two butters will have different textures: the brown butter should be mealy while the regular butter should be in pea-size chunks.

PREPARATION

Sift the flours into the mixing bowl of a stand mixer (recommended) or a large mixing bowl if using a handheld mixer. Add the salt and sugar to the flours, then add the brown butter pieces. Using the paddle attachment, mix on low speed until the butter is in pea-size, mealy pieces. Then add the regular butter and mix until you see the butter forming pea-size pieces. Add the water and vodka mixture all at once and mix on low for 1 to 2 minutes or until the dough just begins to come together.

If you're making the Pecan Pie (page 192), now is the time to par-bake or blind-bake the crust. Divide the dough into 2 equal portions and form into round, flat disks. Wrap and refrigerate 30 minutes to rest. Remove the dough after it's had enough time to chill and roll out into 12-inch circles. Line the pie shells, trim the edges, crimp the edges, and freeze.

Once the dough is frozen, line the interior of the frozen pie shell with parchment paper and fill with pie weights or dried beans. Bake at 350°F for 20 minutes, remove from the oven, and let cool for 5 minutes. Remove the parchment and beans and preheat the oven to 325°F. Return to the oven to dry out the bottom of the pie shell, approximately 5 to 7 minutes.

BROWN BUTTER

YIELD: 4 cups

- 2 pounds of butter

At Buxton, we make brown butter in large batches. At home, it's also easy to make a bit more than you need—then you'll have it on hand to play with in other recipes as well. (If you don't want to make the full amount below, though, you can reduce the batch size.) Making brown butter will get easier with each attempt. You'll learn exactly when to pull it off the heat before it burns. If you take it over the browning point by just a little, give it a taste. If it's a dark chestnut-brown color, it may still be delicious.

PREPARATION

Place the butter in a medium-size pot with a heavy bottom. Over low heat, gently melt the butter. Once the butter has melted, you can raise the heat to medium so that the water will cook out of the butter a bit faster. You may hear or see some splattering—this is a sign that the water is being cooked out of the fat. Eventually the spattering will subside and you will begin to see foaming across the top of the simmering butterfat. This is the time to pay close attention to the color and the browning process.

Swirl the pot slowly to move the foam so that you can easily see the color of the fat below. You can check for the ideal brown color by spooning a little fat onto a light-colored plate. When the color of the fat is a medium brown and the foam smells like toasted milk—rich and nutty—it's finished. The whole process, start to finish, can take anywhere from 10 to 20 minutes for a batch this size, depending on the level of heat.

Remove the pot from the heat and pour the brown butter into a glass, metal, or ceramic container to cool. You can strain the toasted milk solids or leave them in the butter.

BANANA PUDDING PIE

 **YIELD:** One pie
(9 inches)

- ⅓ vanilla bean, seeds scraped from the pod
- ¼ teaspoon vanilla extract
- 1 cinnamon stick
- ⅛ teaspoon (pinch) allspice
- 1¼ cups milk, divided
- ⅓ cup sugar
- 1½ tablespoons all-purpose flour
- ½ teaspoon salt
- 2 egg yolks
- 1½ gelatin sheets or 1½ teaspoons granulated gelatin
- ¼ cup ice-cold water
- 2 ripe bananas, thinly sliced
- 1 Bunilla Wafer Crust (page 186)
- Brown Sugar Meringue (page 187)

Personally, I've never been a big fan of banana pudding—but I do recognize that it's part of just about every classic barbecue restaurant's menu. Unless it's a takeaway-only spot, serving meat by the pound, there's going to be banana pudding on the menu. That's why when Ashley was coming up with our first dessert menu, I told her if she didn't make banana pudding, I was going to make it myself! But Ashley came up with her own unique spin on the classic pudding and the Banana Pudding Pie was born. It's definitely a more labor-intensive and elevated version of banana pudding, but once you try it, you'll agree it's worth the effort.

PREPARATION

Combine the vanilla pod and seeds, vanilla extract, cinnamon stick, and allspice with 1 cup of the milk in a small saucepan, reserving ¼ cup of milk. Heat over medium-high until the mixture almost scalds. Turn off the heat and allow the spices to infuse for 10 minutes.

Meanwhile, in a small mixing bowl, whisk the sugar, flour, and salt together. Add the egg yolks and the reserved ¼ cup of milk and continue to mix until evenly blended.

Set up an ice-water bath in a large bowl or in the sink, and nest a large mixing bowl and strainer in the ice water so you're ready to shock the custard.

While whisking, temper the hot milk mixture into the egg mixture, then return all of the mixture to the pot to thicken over low heat. Stir frequently with a spatula as the mixture thickens. After the

pudding bubbles for 1 minute, switch to a whisk and agitate the thickened custard—this helps smooth out the lumps. Once it tastes like vanilla pudding, it's done. If you taste it and it seems starchy, cook for 1 to 2 more minutes.

Remove the mixture from the heat and begin whisking rapidly to smooth out any lumps. Pour the custard through the strainer into the mixing bowl set in an ice-water bath to stop the cooking process. Cover with plastic wrap to prevent a skin from forming.

As the custard cools, bloom the gelatin. To bloom the granulated gelatin, pour the ¼ cup of ice-cold water into a mixing bowl. Sprinkle all of the gelatin on top of the water. Allow the gelatin to evenly absorb the water for 5 minutes or according to your package directions. If you're using sheet gelatin, plunge each sheet into a bowl of ice water. Allow

recipe continues

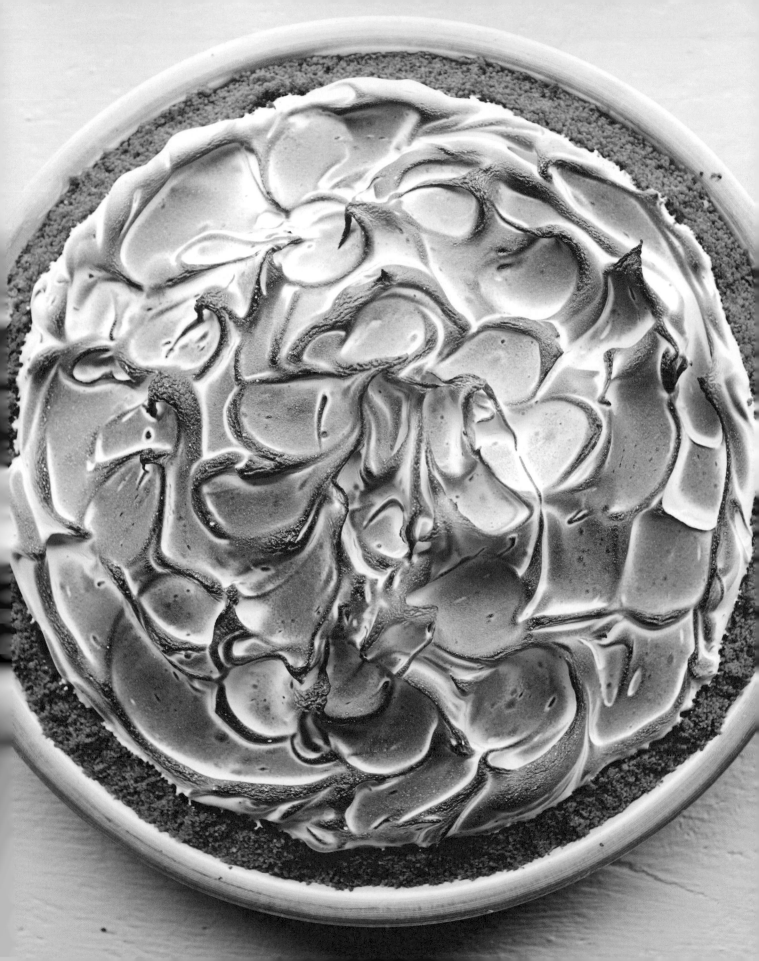

BUNILLA WAFER CRUST

YIELD: 1 shell for 1 pie (9 inches)

- About 30 Bunilla Wafers (page 170), or 4 heaping cups vanilla wafers
- 1 tablespoon light brown sugar
- 2 tablespoons brown butter, melted (page 183), plus 1 to 2 tablespoons extra, as needed
- 1/8 teaspoon salt

Using a food processor, combine and process the wafers until they're broken up into very fine crumbs and appear sandy. You should now have 2 level, packed cups of wafer crumbs—add more wafers if needed.

In a medium mixing bowl, combine the wafers with the brown sugar, melted brown butter, and salt. Mix by hand to blend evenly. The crust should be moist enough to maintain its shape when squeezed by hand. If not, add a little more melted brown butter.

Press the mixture into pie pans, starting at the bottom and finishing with the sides. It will take about 1 1/4 cups to fill each 9-inch pie pan. Pay attention to the depth of the sides and the bottom of the crust. They should all be an even thickness.

Chill the crumb crusts in the pans for at least 10 minutes. Bake at 325°F for 8 to 10 minutes or until they are evenly browned and slightly darker in color.

the sheets to remain in the ice water for 5 minutes, or until the sheets rehydrate (bloom) and are soft, rubbery, and pliable in texture. Remove bloomed sheets from the ice water, squeeze gently to remove any excess water, and transfer to your mixing bowl with ¼ cup ice-cold water.

Once the custard has cooled to 90°F, add one-third of the warm custard to the gelatin bowl and stir to combine and melt the gelatin. Add the rest of the warm custard and stir to blend evenly.

NOTE: If you have trouble incorporating the gelatin into the custard, you can transfer the custard to your blender, then add the warm custard

and gelatin mixture to the blender and blend on medium speed until you have fully combined the custards and the consistency is very smooth. Also, the custard must be warm to melt and mix evenly with the bloomed gelatin.

Add thinly sliced bananas to the gelatinized custard. Use a spatula to ensure bananas are evenly dispersed and coated.

Pour into a prebaked Bunilla Wafer Pie Crust (page 186), cover with plastic wrap pressed tightly against the surface, and refrigerate to set at least 3 hours. You will not bake this pie. Once it's set, you can add the meringue and refrigerate. This pie should be served cold.

BROWN SUGAR MERINGUE

YIELD: enough for one 9-inch pie

- Water
- ¼ teaspoon lemon juice
- ⅛ teaspoon cream of tartar
- 3 egg whites
- ¼ cup tightly packed light brown sugar
- ½ cup sugar

Brown sugar is a natural fit for meringue. In addition to the subtle flavor, which really shines when browned, the brown sugar contains molasses, which is acidic. Meringues hold better with acid—which is why you often see lemon juice in the recipe. But the molasses in the brown sugar helps as well.

PREPARATION

Find a large pot in which you can nest a medium-size mixing bowl. Fill the pot about one-quarter of the way full with water and bring to a simmer.

Get your medium-size mixing bowl and whisk ready, making sure they're super clean and dry. Add the lemon juice and cream of tartar to the bowl. Add the egg whites and sugars. Stir until the mixture is evenly combined. Place the bowl over the simmering water and heat to 165°F. Use a spatula to stir the whites

and sugars frequently while heating to dissolve the sugar.

Pour the heated mixture into the bowl of a stand mixer. Whip on high speed to stiff and shiny peaks.

Transfer the topping to your pie, using a spoon or spatula to spread the topping. Brown the meringue with a culinary torch or just use the broiler in your oven, set on high. Leave the door to the oven cracked while broiling meringue. It will take 3 to 6 minutes depending on your oven.

GRAPE HULL PIE

YIELD: 1 pie (9 inches)

- About 25 to 30 muscadine grapes (once separated, about 2½ cups grape pulp and 2½ cups grape skins)
- 1 tablespoon tapioca starch
- ¼ cup cornstarch
- 1¼ cups sugar
- 2 teaspoons salt
- ¼ teaspoon cinnamon
- ¼ teaspoon cardamom
- ¼ teaspoon powdered ginger
- 2½ teaspoons lemon juice
- ⅔ teaspoon vanilla extract
- 1 Rye Crust, prebaked (page 179)
- Rye Crumble (page 189)

Growing up, my backyard was filled with muscadine grapevines and they're one of the fruits I most associate with my childhood. While talking with my parents about our dessert menu at Buxton, my dad mentioned my grandma's grape hull pies—which I barely remembered. I'd heard of, and eaten, grape pies before, but on muscadines the skins are so tough. I thought it was very interesting that after she juiced the grapes, she found such a great use for the skins. Our version replaces my grandma's meringue with a crumble topping that goes with the rye crust, but feel free to substitute meringue if you'd like. You'll find our recipe on page 187.

PREPARATION
PREPARE THE GRAPES

Start by hulling and processing the grapes, separating the skins into 1 container and the pulp into another. It's okay to leave the seeds in with the pulp for now.

In a small saucepan, cook the pulp and seeds over medium heat. Cook until the pulp has become translucent and the liquid reduces by one-quarter. Strain out the seeds by pouring the pulp through a bowl strainer. Tap the strainer and gently stir with a spoon. The seeds will remain and the pulp will strain through.

Transfer the skins to a food processor and pulse until the skins are broken up into small pieces. Measure out 1¼ cups of skins for the recipe. Discard the remaining skins. Measure 1¼ cups of pulp and combine with the skins in a mixing bowl.

MAKE THE FILLING

In a large bowl, whisk together the tapioca and cornstarch, sugar, salt, and spices. In a small bowl, measure out and combine the lemon juice and vanilla.

Add the pulp and skins to the lemon juice mixture. Stir well to combine. Add the wet to the dry ingredients and stir until the ingredients are thoroughly combined.

Transfer the mixture to a medium-size saucepan and cook the pie filling over medium heat. Stir frequently and cook until it thickens. Usually this will be at just about the point where it starts to bubble. Cool the filling to room temperature in an ice bath. Reserve.

BAKE THE PIE

Transfer the mixture to a cooled (room temperature) prebaked Rye Crust (page 179). Top with the Rye Crumble on page 189. Bake at 350°F for 20 to 25 minutes or until the streusel is brown and the filling is just starting to bubble.

Cool at room temperature for 4 hours before serving.

RYE CRUMBLE

🍴 **YIELD:** 2 cups, enough for 1 pie

- 1 cup rye flour
- 1 cup all-purpose flour
- ½ teaspoon salt
- ¼ cup brown sugar
- ¼ cup granulated sugar
- ¾ cup (1½ sticks) unsalted butter, diced and at room temperature
- ¼ teaspoon ground ginger
- ¾ teaspoon cinnamon

In a medium-size mixing bowl, combine all the ingredients. Pinch and break apart the butter into the dry ingredients. The mixture is combined once small clumps form. Refrigerate for at least 1 hour to chill the butter before using the mixture to top a pie. (Top before baking.)

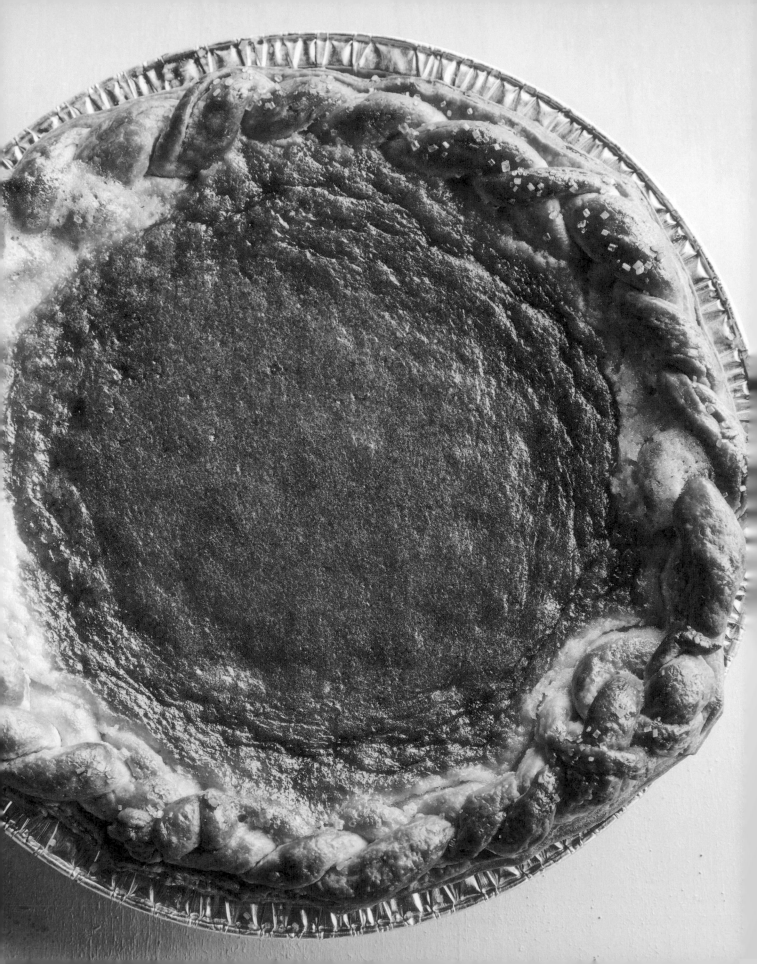

BUTTERMILK PIE

🍴 **YIELD:** 1 pie (9 inches)

- 1¾ cups sugar
- 1 teaspoon salt
- 1 tablespoon pastry flour
- 3 eggs, room temperature
- 1 egg yolk, room temperature
- ¼ cup (½ stick) unsalted butter, melted
- 1 cup buttermilk, room temperature
- 1 tablespoon lime or lemon juice
- 2 teaspoons vanilla extract
- ¼ teaspoon freshly grated nutmeg

NOTE: Make sure all cold ingredients in this recipe are at room temperature as specified, or this pie filling will not mix properly.

- 1 Super Flaky Pie Crust, prebaked and cooled (page 177)

Buttermilk pie is a custard pie, which means the trickiest part of a successful buttermilk pie is cooking it properly. If you overbake it, it will curdle and remind you of overcooked eggs—there will be large, unattractive bubbles. On the other hand, if you underbake it, you'll have a runny pie, and nobody wants that, either. There's a magic moment in between, when you pull the pie out and it is still jiggly in the center—then it sets up as it cools.

The only secret we have besides baking the pie properly is the buttermilk. We use fresh Wholesome Country Creamery buttermilk delivered by Farm to Home Milk here in Asheville. Because the buttermilk is the star of this pie, using high-quality buttermilk is what will give you the bright, tangy flavor. Depending on the season, you can top this pie in different ways. Try fresh peach jam in the summer or pecan brittle in the winter.

PREPARATION
MAKE THE FILLING

Preheat the oven to 350°F. In the bowl of your stand mixer (recommended) or in a large mixing bowl if using a handheld mixer, mix the sugar, salt, and flour with the whisk attachment over low speed to blend evenly. In a separate container, beat the eggs by hand until the whites and yolks are well mixed. Add the eggs slowly to the dry mixture while mixing on low speed.

Continuing on low speed, blend the butter into the mixture. Once the butter is fully incorporated, add the buttermilk and whisk gently. Add the lime or lemon juice, vanilla, and nutmeg; whisk until they're fully integrated with the filling.

BAKE THE PIE

Pour the mixture into a cooled (room-temperature) prebaked Super Flaky Pie Crust (page 177). Bake for 20 minutes at 350°F, then reduce temperature to 325°F and bake for 10 more minutes or until just set—the custard should still be slightly jiggly. Let the pie cool at room temperature for at least 2 hours before slicing and serving.

PECAN PIE

🔪 **YIELD:** 1 pie (9 inches)

- ⅓ cups Brown Butter (page 183), melted
- ½ cup maple syrup
- ½ cup sorghum
- ½ cup corn syrup
- 2 tablespoons sugar
- 1 tablespoon all-purpose flour
- ½ teaspoon salt
- ¼ teaspoon cinnamon
- 3 eggs, whisked well and passed through a sieve (to remove any pieces of egg that are not smooth)
- 1 teaspoon vanilla extract
- 1 cup pecans, lightly toasted and roughly broken
- 1 Brown Butter Crust, par-baked and cooled (page 182)

I don't have a very big sweet tooth, but when the craving strikes, I'm always drawn to sweets with nuts—whether it's a candy bar or chocolate-almond ice cream. If I really think about it, I could probably trace the obsession back to my childhood. My dad loved chocolate-covered pecans, and they were often the only sweets around the house. From there, it's not a far jump to pecan pie, which has always been one of my favorites. I just love the custardy, gooey, nutty filling and the crisp bite of the crust. It's sweet, but also a little savory thanks to the nuts.

PREPARATION

MAKE THE FILLING

Preheat oven to 325°F. Set up 3 small bowls for mixing: one for the sugar syrups, one for the eggs and vanilla, and one for the dry ingredients.

Melt the brown butter in a small saucepan. Turn off the heat once the butter is completely melted and whisk into the maple, sorghum, and corn syrup until evenly combined. Transfer back to a small bowl.

In another small bowl, whisk to combine the sugar, flour, salt, and cinnamon. In the third small bowl, whisk to combine the eggs and vanilla. Add the dry mixture to the egg and vanilla mixture and stir to combine, then combine that mixture into the bowl with the butter and syrup mixture, whisking until well combined.

BAKE THE PIE

Distribute the pecans into a cooled (room-temperature) par-baked Brown Butter Crust (page 182). Pour the mixture into the pie shell on top of the pecans. Bake at 325°F for about 20 minutes, rotating halfway through cooking. The pie is done when it is nearly set and only the center jiggles slightly when moved. Cool at room temperature for at least 6 hours before slicing. Refrigerating the pie for 1 hour after baking will help the pie set more quickly. However, it's best if you make this pie the day before you need to serve it and let it set overnight before slicing.

APPLE CHEDDAR PIE

🍴 **YIELD:** 1 pie (9 inches)

FOR THE DRY MIX

- 1 tablespoon granulated sugar
- 2 tablespoons brown sugar
- ⅛ teaspoon cinnamon
- Pinch ground nutmeg
- Pinch ground ginger
- ⅛ teaspoon salt
- 2 tablespoons cornstarch
- 2 tablespoons tapioca starch
- ⅛ teaspoon malic acid

FOR THE FILLING

- 5 to 6 medium apples (mix varieties)
- Juice of ½ lemon
- ½ cup apple pie dry mix
- 2 tablespoons butter, cold
- Egg wash (1 egg combined with 1 teaspoon cream and a pinch salt, whisked and strained)

FOR THE PIE

- 1 Cheddar Crust recipe, rolled out and chilled according to page 180

Apple pie is the classic American pie, no doubt about it. I'm not sure where the tradition of adding a slice of cheese to the plate before serving it came from, but that's the inspiration for our take on apple pie. For the Buxton version, we bake cheese right into the crust and fill the inside with a variety of local apples. We live right next door to Henderson County, a big apple-producing region, so when apples are in season, we have a great selection. When selecting your own mix, make sure to mix some sweet varieties with some tart ones for a more complex pie. To serve, we heat a slice of cheese on top of a slice of pie using the fire in the pit. But at home you can use a broiler as well.

Two tips when making this pie: First, try to bake it 12 to 24 hours before you plan to slice and serve it. The filling needs time to set up, and if you give it that time, it will slice beautifully. Second, don't mix the filling until right before you're ready to bake. Make sure you have that pie crust ready!

PREPARATION
MAKE THE FILLING

In a small mixing bowl, combine all dry mix ingredients and stir until evenly combined.

Core and peel the apples. Cut into ¼-inch pieces and transfer to a large mixing bowl. Add the lemon juice and ½ cup of the dry mix; toss well to combine.

BAKE THE PIE

In a pie plate lined with one rolled-out Cheddar Crust, layer the apples well, starting on the edges and building from the base to the top. Aim for a tall, compact apple pie.

Pinch the butter into little pieces and scatter on top of the apples. Dampen the edges of the pie crust with about a teaspoon of water. Cover the pie with the chilled, rolled-out dough for the top and press the edges together to adhere. Trim the edges with a knife or scissors to just over the lip of the pie plate. Roll the edges underneath to seal the pie filling inside.

Shape the edges with a fork in a crosshatch pattern. Slash 4 small areas on top to vent. Brush the egg wash evenly over the pie crust and place it in the refrigerator for 15 minutes. Remove from the fridge, brush once more with egg wash, and bake at 375°F for 15 minutes. Reduce the oven temperature to 350°F and continue baking for about 30 minutes or until the crust is completely brown and the filling is gooey and bubbly. Allow to cool at room temperature for 6 to 8 hours before slicing. Letting it cool overnight at room temperature is best.

CHOCOLATE CHESS PIE

YIELD: 1 pie (9 inches)

- ⅓ cup (¾ stick) unsalted butter, melted
- ⅛ cup bittersweet chocolate
- 2¼ eggs (to divide an egg, crack an egg into a small bowl, whisk, and then divide)
- 1 egg yolk
- 1 cup granulated sugar
- 2 tablespoons tightly packed brown sugar
- ¾ teaspoon salt
- 1½ teaspoons cocoa powder
- 1½ teaspoons all-purpose flour
- ⅔ cup buttermilk, room temperature
- ¾ teaspoon vanilla extract
- 1 tablespoon bourbon
- 1 Chocolate Short Crust (page 197), par-baked

Like the Buttermilk Pie (page 191), the most important thing to get right for this pie is the baking time. You need a perfectly set custard for the pie to be at its best. Another similarity to the Buttermilk Pie is that the ingredients you use will make a big difference. Search for fresh, local buttermilk; buy high-quality chocolate and cocoa powder; and use the same quality of bourbon that you would drink. When the pie is ready, pair it with a strong cup of black coffee for an unforgettable dessert.

PREPARATION
MAKE THE FILLING

Preheat the oven to 350°F. Using a double boiler or *bain marie*, melt the butter and the chocolate gently until they reach a smooth consistency. While this mixture melts, whisk the eggs in a small bowl until they are also smooth. Add the sugars and salt to the eggs and whisk until they are uniform in texture (no egg pieces).

In a large mixing bowl, use a whisk to blend the cocoa and the flour. Add the melted butter and chocolate mixture, buttermilk, vanilla extract, and bourbon; whisk to combine. Whisk in the egg and sugar mixture until evenly blended.

BAKE THE PIE

Transfer the mixture to a cooled (room temperature) par-baked Chocolate Short Crust (page 197). Bake at 350°F for about 20 minutes, rotate, and bake another 15 minutes or until the pie is set overall but jiggly in the center. Cool at room temperature for 3 hours before slicing and serving.

CHOCOLATE SHORT CRUST

YIELD: 1 shell for 1 pie (9 inches)

- 2 tablespoons sugar
- ½ teaspoon salt
- ⅓ cup unsalted butter, room temperature
- 1 egg yolk
- ¼ teaspoon vanilla extract
- 1¼ cups bread flour
- 1½ tablespoons cocoa

In a stand mixer (recommended) or in a large mixing bowl with a handheld mixer, paddle the sugar, salt, butter, egg, and vanilla on low speed until blended. Scrape down frequently and try to avoid incorporating air.

Sift the flour and cocoa powder together and add them to the butter mixture. Mix on low speed for 2 minutes, until smooth and evenly mixed. Remove the dough from the mixer and place it on top of a piece of plastic wrap. You can use a spatula if the dough is a little sticky. Wrap the dough in the plastic wrap and shape it into a round disk. Refrigerate for 1 hour or until chilled.

After chilling, remove the plastic wrap and place the dough between two sheets of parchment paper (for clean and tidy rolling), or flour the counter lightly and begin rolling the chilled dough directly on the floured counter.

Roll the dough into an 11- to 12-inch circle. (This diameter will fully line a 9-inch pan.) Carefully place the dough into the pie pan. If the dough gets too warm during rolling, chill it again for a little while to a workable temperature.

Line the pie pan and trim the edges. If there are any tears, gently press the dough together and even it out. Freeze the lined pie shell until firm.

Preheat the oven to 375°F. Line the interior of the frozen pie shell with parchment paper and fill with pie weights or dried beans. Bake at 375°F for 10 minutes, then reduce the temperature to 350°F and bake for 15 minutes. Remove from the oven and let cool for 5 minutes. Remove the parchment and beans, then fill and bake according to the recipe.

CHERRY YUM YUM PIE

 YIELD: 1 pie (9 inches)

FOR THE GRAHAM CRACKER CRUST

- 4 tablespoons melted butter
- 1½ cups fine graham cracker crumbs (see page 174 for our Graham Crackers recipe)

FOR THE FILLING

- 2 sheets of gelatin, or 2 teaspoons granulated gelatin
- ¼ cup ice-cold water
- 1 cup cream, heated to 120°F
- ¼ teaspoon salt
- 2 teaspoons orange zest
- 1 tablespoon lemon juice
- ⅓ cup sugar
- 2 egg yolks
- ¼ cup milk
- ¾ cup cream cheese, room temperature
- ½ cup sour cream or crème fraîche
- 1 teaspoon vanilla extract

Different variations of cherry yum yum have long been a childhood favorite for many in the South—just a bite and you'll know how it got that name. For our Cherry Yum Yum Pie, we use our house graham crackers for the crumb crust, a cheesecake batter in the middle, and a fresh cherry filling on top. If you're short on time, you can certainly try substituting store-bought graham crackers or cherry topping. Many a grandmother has done the same, so you know there's no shame in the shortcut.

PREPARATION

MAKE THE GRAHAM CRACKER CRUST

Preheat your oven to 325°F. In a small mixing bowl, add the melted butter to the graham cracker crumbs. Mix evenly by hand. When you squeeze a handful of the mixture, it should clump easily and hold its shape. If it's still too crumbly, add a little more melted butter.

Press the mixture evenly into the sides and bottom of the pie pan. Chill for 10 minutes and then bake at 325°F for 10 to 12 minutes, or until the crust is toasted. Cool completely at room temperature before filling. Once the crust is cool, add the filling you'll make in the next section.

MAKE THE FILLING

To bloom the granulated gelatin, pour ¼ cup of ice-cold water into the mixing bowl. Sprinkle all of the gelatin granules on top of the cold water. Allow the gelatin to evenly absorb the water for 5 minutes or according to your package directions. If you're using sheet gelatin, plunge each sheet into a bowl of ice water. Allow the sheets to remain in the ice water for 5 minutes, or until the sheets rehydrate (bloom) and are soft, rubbery, and pliable in texture. Remove bloomed sheets from the ice water, squeeze gently to remove any excess water, and transfer to your mixing bowl with ¼ cup ice-cold water.

In a blender, combine the gelatin, hot cream, salt, zest, lemon juice, and sugar. Blend on low speed for about 1 minute, or until everything is very well incorporated. Add the yolks, milk, cream cheese, sour cream (or crème

recipe continues

- ½ cup sugar, divided
- 1 teaspoon tapioca starch
- 1 tablespoon cornstarch
- ¼ teaspoon salt
- 1 cup cold water
- ½ cup orange juice
- ½ vanilla bean, split and scraped
- 1 teaspoon almond extract
- 2 cups cherries, washed, stemmed, pitted, halved
- 2 tablespoons butter

fraîche), and vanilla extract. Blend on low speed for 2 minutes. Feel free to increase the speed a little if you see some unincorporated pieces of cream cheese.

Pour into the cooled graham cracker crust and refrigerate for at least 2 hours, or until the filling is completely set.

MAKE THE TOPPING

While the filling starts to set, make the cherry topping, as it will have to cool as well before you add it to the pie.

In a small mixing bowl, whisk half the sugar, starches, and salt with the cold water. In a small saucepan, add the juice, vanilla, almond extract, and remaining sugar. Bring the mixture to a simmer to dissolve the sugar completely. Whisk the hot syrup into the water and dry ingredient mixture, then add everything back to the saucepan. Bring to a simmer over medium heat. Add the cherries and cook for 2 minutes. Remove the pan from the heat, add the butter, and stir to dissolve. Cool the cherry topping completely in the fridge. Once cool, pour on top of the chilled pie and serve.

BUXTON'S POUND CAKE

YIELD: 1 small loaf

FOR THE PAN

- Butter to coat
- ¼ cup sugar

FOR THE CAKE

- 2⅔ cups cake flour
- ⅓ teaspoon baking powder
- ⅓ teaspoon salt
- ⅔ cup (1 stick plus 3⅓ tablespoons) unsalted butter, at room temperature
- ¼ cup shortening
- 2 cups plus 1 tablespoon sugar
- 1 vanilla bean, seeds scraped from the pod
- 4 eggs, room temperature
- 2½ teaspoons vanilla extract
- 2½ teaspoons almond extract
- ¾ cup buttermilk, room temperature

Pound cake is a classic dessert that can be dressed up according to season. It's a great companion for berries and other fruits, in particular. At Buxton, we also like baking the pound cake on the slightly underdone side. There's a very small window when you bake a pound cake where it's set and done but there's a beautiful streak from the top to the center. It's actually referred to as "the sad streak," but we're not sure why that's the case. It seems to us that most people find that streak the best part of the pound cake!

PREPARATION

Preheat your oven to 300°F and liberally butter your loaf pan. Coat the buttered pan with ¼ cup sugar and tilt to make sure sugar is coating the butter. Refrigerate the pan until you're ready to use it.

Combine flour with baking powder and salt by sifting 3 times into a large mixing bowl. In your stand mixer bowl (recommended) or a large mixing bowl, combine the butter and shortening; cream with the mixer for about 10 minutes, until smooth and light. Add the sugar gradually, along with the vanilla seeds, and blend with your mixer on medium speed until light and fluffy, pausing to scrape down the bowl a few times.

In a third bowl, combine the eggs, extracts, and buttermilk. Whisk to mix well. Using the creamed sugar mixture as the master mixing bowl, alternate additions of the dry flour mixture and the wet buttermilk mixture to the master bowl while mixing on low speed. You should add them as follows: dry, wet, dry, wet, dry.

Once it's well combined, remove the mixer bowl from the stand and manually fold the batter to eliminate any streaks. Transfer to the sugared baking pan and bake at 300°F for 15 minutes. After 15 minutes, increase the oven temperature to 325°F and bake for 45 minutes or until the cake is golden brown and feels barely set in the center.

Remove the cake from the oven and let it cool for 20 minutes. Carefully invert the pan and continue to cool the cake on a wire baking rack. The cake will keep for about a week in a well-sealed container at room temperature.

photo on opposite page

ACKNOWLEDGMENTS

I would be a fool if I didn't start this list with my wife—Jennifer Sellers when we first started dating sixteen years ago, now Jennifer Moss. She has been through it all, patiently letting me chase my dream. Thank you for believing in me. Now let's chase your dream.

Thanks to my folks, Terrell and Debbie Moss, for introducing me to so many influential people, things, and places. Thanks also for inspiring me and encouraging me to follow my dreams—and for letting me be a weirdo when I was a little kid. I love you both.

To my grand folks, Hubert and Mildred Moore and R.T. and Jessie Moss: I wouldn't be in the barbecue business if it wasn't for you. You infused my life with your traditions, independent spirits, and the love of feeding and nourishing people.

Thanks to Meherwan and Molly Irani for taking a leap of faith and for wanting to get on the wild ride we call Buxton Hall Barbecue.

Thank you, Ashley Capps, for always pushing me, inspiring me, and totally destroying it in the Buxton bakery. I owe you so much. This book wouldn't have happened without all of your countless hours and hard work. Thanks you for being there since the very beginning.

Sarah Cousler and Dan Silo, thank you for following me around, believing in me, and waiting so long for Buxton to open. Thank you so much for all of your dedication and all the hard work and long hours you put in. You helped build the bones of Buxton, literally. I can't wait to help you build your own places.

Johnny and Charlotte Autry, thank you for taking such great pictures and making our food look so good.

I also can't thank the entire Buxton Family enough. You are Buxton Hall Barbecue. I love you all, and thanks for all of your smiling faces and hard work.

Thanks to all the Moores and the Mosses, all of my friends, all the local Ashevillians who have been so supporting of my journey, all the customers who have walked through the doors so far, Ashley Turner, Nicole McConville, Mikey Files, Kyle Beach, Joy Clayton, Charlotte Fahy, Michael Moore, Brian Canipelli, Nate Allen, Bryan Furman, Andy Lee, Keia Mastrianni, Jed Portman, Rodney Scott, Sam Jones, Alvin Diec, Maggie White, Derek Watson, David Modaff, Gra Moore, Larry and Kathleen Crocker, All Souls Pizza, The Double Crown, Kimball House, Burial Beer Co., and everyone else I've forgotten who has helped me along the way. I could keep going forever.

Last, thanks to Thom O'Hearn and the rest of the Quarto team for putting up with a first-time author's trials and tribulations.

Thank you all.

INDEX

ABOUT THE AUTHOR

Elliott Moss has received national attention for his innovative cooking from the *New York Times*, *Food & Wine*, *Martha Stewart Living*, *Southern Living*, *Bon Appétit*, *Garden & Gun*, *GQ*, and other publications. He was nominated for a James Beard Award for Best Chef Southeast in 2013. He currently resides in Asheville, North Carolina, where he has been the head chef at the celebrated restaurant the Admiral and pop-up restaurants such as Punk Wok and the Thunderbird. He is now the co-owner and head chef of Buxton Hall Barbecue.